**Penelope Deutscher** is Associate Professor of Philosophy at Northwestern University. Her books on twentieth-century French philosophy and philosophy of gender include *Yielding Gender: Feminism, Deconstruction and the History of Philosophy*, *A Politics of Impossible Difference: The Later Work of Luce Irigaray*, and the anthologies: *Enigmas: Essays on Sarah Kofman* (co-edited with Kelly Oliver) and *Repenser le politique: l'apport du féminisme* (co-edited with Françoise Collin).

of Hospitality Derrida 2000
P. 67

philosophy of impossibility p 69

< use in class p. 83
Hobi Bhabha

p. 84 British in India
p. 84 & Bible

impossibility of perfecting
yet need to go on
mon amor p. 85

# HOW TO READ

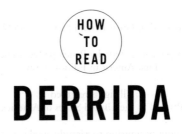

# HOW `TO READ

# DERRIDA

## PENELOPE DEUTSCHER

W. W. Norton & Company
New York   London

First published in Great Britain by Granta Publications

Copyright © 2005 by Penelope Deutscher
First American Edition 2006

For information about permission to reproduce selections from this book,
write to Permissions, W. W. Norton & Company, Inc.,
500 Fifth Avenue, New York, NY 10110

Manufacturing by The Maple-Vail Book Manufacturing Group
Production manager: Amanda Morrison

Library of Congress Cataloging-in-Publication Data

Deutscher, Penelope, 1966–
How to read Derrida / Penelope Deutscher.— 1st American ed.
p. cm. — (How to read)
Includes bibliographical references and index.
ISBN-13: 978-0-393-32879-0 (pbk.)
ISBN-10: 0-393-32879-1 (pbk.)
1. Derrida, Jacques. I. Title. II. How to read (New York, N.Y.)
B2430.D484D49 2006
194—dc22
2005035278

W. W. Norton & Company, Inc.
500 Fifth Avenue, New York, N.Y. 10110
www.wwnorton.com

W. W. Norton & Company Ltd.
Castle House, 75/76 Wells Street, London W1T 3QT

1 2 3 4 5 6 7 8 9 0

# CONTENTS

## SERIES EDITOR'S FOREWORD

## How am I to read *How to Read*?

This series is based on a very simple, but novel idea. Most beginners' guides to great thinkers and writers offer either potted biography or condensed summaries of their major works, or perhaps even both. *How to Read*, by contrast, brings the reader face-to-face with the writing itself in the company of an expert guide. Its starting point is that in order to get close to what a writer is all about, you have to get close to the words they actually use and be shown how to read those words.

Every book in the series is in a way a masterclass in reading. Each author has selected ten or so short extracts from a writer's work and looks at them in detail as a way of revealing their central ideas and thereby opening doors onto a whole world of thought. Sometimes these extracts are arranged chronologically to give a sense of a thinker's development over time, sometimes not. The books are not merely compilations of a thinker's most famous passages, their 'greatest hits', but rather they offer a series of clues or keys that will enable readers to go on and make discoveries of their own. In addition to the texts and readings, each book provides a short biographical chronology and suggestions for further reading, internet resources, and so on. The books in the *How to Read* series don't claim to tell you all you need to know about Freud, Nietzsche and Darwin, or indeed Shakespeare and the Marquis de Sade, but they do offer the best starting point for further exploration.

Unlike the available second-hand versions of the minds that have shaped our intellectual, cultural, religious, political and scientific landscape, *How to Read* offers a refreshing set of first-hand encounters with those minds. Our hope is that these books will, by turn, instruct, intrigue, embolden, encourage and delight.

Simon Critchley
New School for Social Research, New York

## ACKNOWLEDGEMENTS

Many thanks to Cristina, Michael and Pip for advice and help; to Simon for the suggestion; and, at Granta, to Bella for her strenuous copyediting, to Colette for her patience and precision, and to George.

# INTRODUCTION

In 2004, the office of the French president Jacques Chirac announced the death at seventy-four years of age of the philosopher Jacques Derrida, 'one of the major figures in the intellectual life of our time'. Internationally, he was widely considered the most important French philosopher of the late twentieth century. He published over forty works, was the subject of two movies and a number of media controversies, and had an impact on a remarkable number of disciplines and areas of study including, to name a few: education, gender, law, literature, mathematics, politics, psychology, race and theology. 'Deconstruction', a term that he coined, is included in French and Anglo-American dictionaries, and turned up in a movie by Woody Allen, a pop song by Scritti Politi, and as an architectural and a fashion style. Not since existentialism has philosophy produced work with this degree of cross-disciplinary and popular appeal.

As a Jewish adolescent in Algeria in the 1940s, during and after the anti-Semitic French colonial régime under German occupation, Jacques Derrida passionately read classical and avant-garde French writers and philosophers: from Rousseau through to Gide, Valéry and Camus, from Kierkegaard through to Nietzsche, Heidegger and Sartre, and he hoped to be a writer. He trained as a philosopher in Paris. One enters the French academic system as a university teacher, not primarily with a doctoral qualification but by passing a competitive state examination. A doctorate typically follows (for this Derrida presented what would become *Of Grammatology* in 1967) and then a second doctorate (*thèse d'état*). Derrida's *thèse d'état* would not be presented until twenty-three years later. He intended it, he quipped, to be his 'last thesis defence'.

This delay, and the 'thesis defence' of an internationally famous philosopher in his fifties, is consistent with Derrida's troubled and ambivalent relationship with academic institutions. Top of his class, he had been excluded in his youth from his school after it reduced the quotas for Jews to seven per cent. Confronted with violent racism, he would avoid school during the period that he was obliged to attend a school for Jewish students and teachers. On his return he was (as he later described himself) a badly behaved student preoccupied with soccer who failed his final school examination on his first try. But he did well enough in his second attempt to be admitted to France's most elite stream within its tertiary education system.

His subsequent experiences as a young student in Paris were isolated and unhappy. Intermittent depression, nervous anxiety and a seesaw between sleeping tablets and amphetamines resulted in exam failures in 1950, 1951 and 1955. But his first published work – an introductory essay that accompanied his 1962 translation of German philosopher Edmund Husserl's *Origin of Geometry* focusing on the importance of language and difference to Husserlian 'ideality' – won the Jean Cavailles Prize. Within two years, his interests in the interconnection between philosophy and literature had taken shape in his work, and combined with his frequent stylistic experimentation, confirmed his reputation for non-conventional academic work.

Though his earliest work on Husserl was well received by

philosophers, many would soon express their reservations. Derrida was writing at a time in academia of acute preoccupation with the maintenance of disciplinary boundaries. Derrida argued that the boundaries could not be rigorously maintained, and his own work flagrantly broke them. While a renowned figure in France and around the world he was also a maverick.

The swings between his early dramatic failures and stellar successes were later mirrored by reactions to his worldwide fame when he was both lauded and denounced internationally. Compare his obituaries – while one piece in the *Guardian* was comprehensive, accurate and respectful, another in the *New York Times* was so scathing it provoked the protests of more than 4000 signatories. Derrida was recognized with many academic honours: the Nietzsche Prize, the Adorno Prize and many honorary university degrees. But when that particular honour was bestowed by Cambridge it was contested by some fellows of the university. The French president may have done him the honour of announcing his death, but Derrida had also been denied certain posts in the French public university system during his lifetime, and had never had an easy relationship with the French academic establishment.

Another obituary compared the words of René Wellek, for whom Derrida had encouraged the destruction of 'the very concepts of knowledge and truth' (Welleck 2005, 44), with the words of Peggy Kamuf, for whom he had 'offered a way to perform serious intellectual work in the humanities while maintaining "that urgency of response to the abuses of power" which fed political engagement' (McLemee 2004). The reader of *How to Read Derrida* is likely to have a similarly bifurcated relationship to his work. Some will be intrigued by his style and his way of reading, just as others will resist what seems either nonsensical or impractical. Derrida might have agreed with Drucilla Cornell and Judith Butler that 'there is nothing radical about common sense' (Butler 1999, xviii). Because he liked to make the familiar new and strange, it wasn't surprising that his work was controversial.

Deconstruction is often thought of as a dismantling, or undoing. Certainly, Derrida thought that an argument, an individual or an institution's account of itself was not necessarily the most reliable authority. The moment we are confronted with self-representations, Derrida thought we should hone our listening and our critical faculties, a little like a highly attentive therapist or psychoanalyst. Deconstruction suggests that texts and arguments with which we are most familiar contain hidden and unexpected reserves, points of inner resistance, dialogues and alternatives. Attending to these, Derrida converted our understanding of the available resources of the familiar. Deconstruction was sometimes thought of as a negative or even a nihilist movement. Derrida stressed instead that it was an affirmative and potentially transformative way of reading.

# 1

## DECONSTRUCTIVE READING

The purity of the inside can only be restored if the *charges are brought home* against exteriority as a supplement, inessential yet harmful to the essence, a surplus that *ought* never to have come to be added to the untouched plenitude of the inside. The restoration of internal purity must then reconstitute . . . that to which the *pharmakon* should not have had to be added and attached like a *literal parasite*: a *letter* installing itself inside a living organism to rob it of its *nourishment* . . . In order to cure the latter of the *pharmakon* and rid it of the parasite, it is thus necessary to put the outside back in its place. To keep the outside out. Writing must then return to being what it *should never have ceased to be*: an accessory, and accident, an excess.

Extract from Derrida 1981A, 128

This extract from *Dissemination* serves as a challenging example of what reading Derrida can be like. Derrida is describing a context in which something threatens the purity of some kind of 'inside'. Much of Derrida's work refers to ideals of purity in religion, philosophy, public policy and genetics, and many other domains. Though we can't tell from the above passage, he is suspicious of such ideals.

In *Dissemination*, Derrida is describing a preoccupation with purity in the work of the ancient Greek philosopher Plato. He is interested in how we can change the heritage of ideas we inherit, so his work often responds to other writers and philosophers, who undergo a reinvention in his hands. Derrida's career began with interpretations of figures from the history of philosophy and twentieth-century literature, although we'll see that much of his later work discusses everyday problems and politics. Starting to read Derrida involves us in a kind of double trouble: we must understand both Derrida and Plato.

Yet ideals of purity are commonplace today as they were for Plato. In the 'war on drugs', Derrida claims that 'we find a desire to reconstitute . . . the "ideal body", the "perfect body". A pure body would be a drug-free body.' Derrida encourages us to interrogate and scrutinize the coherence of this ideal. We might conclude that the pure body which is imagined as an ideal doesn't exist. Our bodies never have an 'organic and originary naturalness' (Derrida 1995B, 244). Our bodies have always been exposed to the toxins of the environment; they've ingested and incorporated all sorts of legal yet 'unnatural' materials and substances. This is not to defend drug use in sports, nor to make an apology for all drugs and toxins. But we should pay closer attention to our tendency to debase certain kinds of bodies – those ingesting illegal drugs – in tandem with our elevation of a phantom ideal – a drug-free body. We might find many good reasons to prohibit certain drugs and toxins, but Derrida suggests those reasons shouldn't include the false alibi that a natural body is achievable.

Derrida thinks we repeatedly elevate phantom ideals of origin and purity. A natural, toxin-free body is just one example. We think of this body as threatened. Since toxins are thought of as artificial, exterior contaminants of a body, let's say that an opposition between inside and outside has been constructed. Questions arise such as: 'How can the purity of the inside be restored?' The obvious answer seems to be through drug prohibition. Media and politics tell us that purity can be restored if, as Derrida puts it, 'the charges are brought home against exteriority as a supplement'.

Derrida does not think that purity can ever be restored. Prohibition and devaluation of exterior toxins is a means, not of protecting purity, but the *idea* of purity. Drugs give us something to blame, averting our attention from a question of whether there could ever be a 'natural' body. Are not all bodies always non-natural or contaminated in some way (by pollutants, non 'natural' food and drink, medicines, medical interventions, the requirement that we conform to socially acceptable behaviour, for example)? The elevation of an ideal is a kind of lazy shortcut. A far more complex question is which drugs and which toxins, which interventions and modifications we will accept, which we will exclude, and on what grounds? If the relevant ideal is open to question, as Derrida suggested the pure body was, we must grapple with a responsibility we might prefer to avoid. The question is not 'whether' we'll embrace a contaminated body but *which* contaminants? Derrida believes we should ask questions that probe the phantom ideals implicitly at work in a specific cultural, historical, political or literary context. Are these coherent, possible, or illusory? Do we acknowledge or disavow their incoherent nature? What kind of responsibility comes with acknowledging the impossibility of those ideals?

We start to read like Derrida when we notice that something is deemed potentially pure (such as nature, cultural identity, origin, God). Perhaps a speaker or writer evokes an ideal of purity or perhaps we sense it only indirectly, through the speed with which some terms or individuals are deemed unnatural or threatening. Derrida names this threat the 'other'. Typically, we are told both that the other is no threat at all to the ideal in question, and that it is. Drugs are sometimes seen as threatening to the natural body, but if so, this would call into question the coherence of the 'natural body' in the name of which drugs are denounced. In other words, if the idea of the natural body is fluid, perhaps there is no natural body? Sometimes this produces an unstable, ambivalent argument, one that both decries and denies the threat that the 'other' is said to pose. The media debate commonly queries the scientific or technological remaking of the natural body, at the same time as regretting unnatural substance abuse. But what, and where, is the natural body in the name of which we devalue the unnatural? Is physical training, a specialized diet, being surrounded by minders and keepers, legal chemical and medical intervention, physiotherapy, the capacity for modern-day surgery, natural? How is the natural body defined? Has it ever existed? It existed – someone might reply – perhaps in prehistoric times. But even in a mythical prehistorical society, some substances and environments might be considered unnatural for a body: foodstuffs brought from an unfamiliar area, new forms of agriculture, new ideas about what can be eaten. What makes the toxin of a plant natural or unnatural to the human body that eats it? If the devaluation of the unnatural is not interrogated in tandem with questioning the coherence of the concept of nature, such an argument is described by Derrida as deconstructible. One meaning of this is that it can be broken down and taken apart to expose its weakness, because an idealization of nature may be at work that will not stand up to scrutiny.

Consider another everyday example. New technologies involving surrogate pregnancies are sometimes said to have confused maternity. When it is claimed that the immediate, maternal bond has been disrupted by contemporary technologies allowing a foetus to grow in the womb of a non-biological mother, it is implied that something otherwise 'natural' is perverted by modern technology. The 'other' here is technology, in the form of surrogacy. The threatened purity is natural maternity. If we read this deconstructively, we would ask whether the maternal bond has ever been as natural as all that: 'the mother has always been a matter of interpretation, of social construction' (Derrida 1997A, 27). Throughout history, maternity has always been understood through variable cultural meanings: religious significance, the father's prestige, the cosy domestic hearth, positive clichés of wisdom and grace, negative clichés of need and dependency. The nature of maternity has always been cultural. Derrida suspects that nostalgia for a supposedly natural motherhood is reinforced by the belief that it is now threatened by technology. The belief stops us thinking critically. The complexity of maternity isn't new, and it has always been our problem. Our responsibility is both to acknowledge that complexity and to think about the different ways that maternity has always been interpreted and constructed.

Deconstruction is a term that Derrida invented, and is now included in the standard French dictionary, the *Robert*. *Déconstruction* was originally Derrida's translation of a term used by the twentieth-century German philosopher Martin Heidegger, *Destruktion*. Derrida's practice of borrowing and appropriating terms or fragments of ideas from other historical figures can make it hard to pin down his original ideas.

To understand deconstruction better we can turn to Derrida's definitions of the term, particularly in his later work, such as the roundtable discussion *Deconstruction in a Nutshell*. Derrida's writings not only address how we read philosophical works of, say, Plato and Aristotle, but also engage with contemporary ideas about democracy. These projects are connected; Plato and Aristotle offer some of the earliest ideas about democracy, and the influence of that heritage is still at work on us today:

> The way I tried to read Plato, Aristotle, and others, is not a way of commanding, repeating, or conserving this heritage. It is an analysis which tries to find out how their thinking works or does not work, to find the tensions, the contradictions, the heterogeneity within their own corpus . . . What is the law of this self-deconstruction, this 'auto-deconstruction'? Deconstruction is not a method or some tool that you apply to something from the outside . . . Deconstruction is something which happens and which happens inside; there is a deconstruction at work within Plato's texts, for instance. As my colleagues know, each time I study Plato I try to find some heterogeneity in his own corpus and to see how, for instance, within the *Timaeus* the theme of the *khôra* is incompatible with this supposed system of Plato. So, to be true to Plato, and this is a sign of love and respect for Plato, I have to analyse the functioning and disfunctioning of his work . . . I would say the same for democracy . . . (Derrida 1997A, 9–10)

Perhaps, unlike Derrida, we won't find ourselves reading Plato or Aristotle every day, but we will encounter references to democracy in the morning paper. We might read, as Derrida points out in *Rogues*, that in the name of protecting democracy a popular election was suspended in Algeria so as to protect it against the democratic election of a fundamentalist regime. This kind of incompatibility of ideas might catch our eyes. A critical nose for phantom ideals (in this case, an idealized version of democracy) might provoke in us a new kind of ethics in which new obligations and decisions press on us. We might not oppose the decision taken in Algeria in this instance, but we might nonetheless be wary of the contradictory ideas involved in a suspension of democracy in the name of democracy.

The starting point for deconstruction was the discussion of language in the history of philosophy, particularly the hierarchy of speech over writing. Speech is traditionally preferred over writing because writing seems to derive from speech. According to Aristotle's *On Interpretation*, spoken words are the symbols of mental experience, while written words are the secondary symbols of spoken words (Derrida 1997B, 30), and therefore more removed from mental experience. Plato also valued speech over writing, because in his view it is closer to 'logos', knowledge or reason. Writing is described metaphorically by Plato as an orphaned son, at risk of being out of the proximity and control of its 'father', the author. If a speaker is asked to explain, they are present to authenticate, elaborate on or simply to bring life to their words. If we interrogate written words, they maintain, according to Plato, a most 'majestic silence'. Many linguists and philosophers have preferred to think of language primarily in terms of the spoken rather than the written.

For less technical reasons this preference is sometimes expressed in contemporary culture. If you are called to give evidence in court, it won't do to send a letter, nor to read out loud a statement in court. The actual presence of the speaker and their spontaneously spoken statement is required. In a 2005 retrial in Lake Charles, Louisiana of Wilbert Rideau who had been convicted in 1961 for the murder of a bank worker, stand-ins were asked to 'read the parts' of the testimony of thirteen original witnesses, many of whom had since died. It was felt that the spoken version could add 'life' and authenticity that the written discourse might lack.

Some arguments found in philosophers as ancient as Plato about the value of speech over writing remain with us today. In Plato's *Phaedrus* it is argued that written documents may appear to remedy the limitations of memory but actually threaten it. When we rely on written aids, memory works less hard and may become feeble. Writing is described by the Greek term *pharmakon*. In the opening excerpt, Derrida refers to the *pharmakon,* noting that it embodies the purportedly destructive risks of writing. In ancient Greek, *pharmakon* had multiple meanings and can be translated either as 'poison' or 'remedy'. The *Phaedrus* asks whether writing is a remedy for bad memory or a poison to memory. Today also, we might expect that someone who knows a subject thoroughly can speak spontaneously about it. We are not convinced if they only possess written notes. If they rely on such notes, we might, in agreement with the *Phaedrus* argument, consider that writing is a hindrance, not a help. Perhaps we too think that writing is a *pharmakon*: both a help and a hindrance.

Reading these ambivalent devaluations of writing with a deconstructive eye, we see that the *Phaedrus* evokes an ideal which is at apparent risk from writing (just as surrogacy apparently threatens 'natural' motherhood, and drugs apparently threaten 'natural' bodies). We must ask whether speech has ever guaranteed the knowledge, or the testimonial value, apparently threatened by writing and whether we can dislodge the mystique, and the apparent promise of speech. Returning to spoken testimony in trials, someone relating his or her evidence in person is not necessarily persuasive. Wilbert Rideau was released, despite the prosecution's attempt to re-animate the voices of those who had given evidence against him. Returning to Plato, it is possible to not fully understand facts one can recount. When it is a matter of competency, someone might speak persuasively of a knowledge they have merely learnt by rote. In other words, many of the terms through which writing is devalued – non-reliability, lack of conviction, the absence of an animate persuasiveness or indeed the absence of true knowledge – also apply to much speech. Derrida argued that speech is definable in similar terms to writing, though it is posited as primary to it. Similarly, we saw previously that 'natural' bodies are definable in terms similar to 'drugged' bodies as they both ingest artificial toxins, and 'unnatural motherhood' is definable in terms similar to natural motherhood as both are a matter of social construction and interpretation. The hierarchies between the terms natural and unnatural, pure and contaminated, certain and uncertain, are, on closer inspection, unstable.

Plato's *Phaedrus* claims that speech is closer to the live, physical presence of the individual conveying ideas. Thought or ideas, knowledge or truth, is considered the 'original' position. Derrida countered that although writing might be deemed a copy of speech, speech is a *kind* of writing. If we define writing as the inscription of a communicated idea the mind itself can count as a psychic material in which ideas are inscribed. The *Phaedrus* claims that speech is actually a kind of 'psychic inscription' of ideas, that it is written in the soul of the learner. Today too, it's not uncommon to believe that facts can be mentally 'burnt' by saying them out loud, or to a friend. It seems that speaking ideas out loud registers them more thoroughly in our mind. Yet Derrida is right that we just as commonly think that speech does not, after all, guarantee immediacy with consciousness. I might find myself dissatisfied by the way that my speech communicates my ideas – my spoken words can seem to 'slip out of my control', just as my written words can. I might tell you that what I say is not quite what I meant, or I might find myself surprised by what I say. What is attributed to 'writing' must also be attributed to 'speech': in both there is some delay, some lack of satisfaction, some possible discrepancy from what is imagined as the originating idea, or consciousness. If 'writing' is devalued as a form of communication beyond the control of the originating speaker, and a form that only imperfectly renders one's thought, then speech can also be included under this definition. Speech, from that perspective, can be considered a form of 'writing'.

We have arrived at one of the controversial, and apparently nonsensical views for which Derrida first became well-known in the 1970s: that speech is writing. Considering the ways writing can be devalued in relation to speech, we can see that writing and speech actually have a good deal in common. Derrida's point is to question the idealization of speech, which he thinks throws up mirages of promised immediacy, certainty and presence. The belief that Derrida prefers writing over speech is mistaken. He is suspicious only of the idealization of speech because it involves a phantom promise of the natural, the pure, the original. To direct our attention to those phantom promises Derrida offers us a complex definition of writing that can be hard to follow.

Derrida pursues his argument to its further point, defining 'writing' so that it refers not to writing *per se*, but to *the reasons for its devaluation*. In Plato's philosophy, writing is devalued as distant from a source, secondary, and possibly deceptive. A phantom ideal is at work here, since Derrida finds that speech is *also* deemed by Plato on occasion as distant from a source – of thought, for example – secondary, and carrying the possibility of deception. Plato, in his argument about rote learning, admits that speech is no sure thing: that it is secondary to a thinking psyche, and it too can deceive. In Derrida's view, Plato's description of writing extends to speech, which Derrida concludes is a form of writing.

This is the kind of manoeuvre some have deemed deconstructive trickery or tomfoolery. Derrida invents a name to describe this 'general' writing which covers the broad field of anything to which the devaluation of 'literal' writing (words on the page) must also apply. This term is 'general' or 'generalized' or the 'general economy of' writing, or 'archi-writing', where the prefix 'archi' connotes a sense of pre-eminence and originality – at the beginning is writing, in Derrida's 'general' sense. To describe speech as a form of archi-writing, is to say that despite its phantom promise it is not immediate and embodies the possibility of deception. Derrida's real point here is that this is true of *all* forms of language: this fear is the original condition of language. By his expanded definition, all forms of language can be described as 'forms of writing'. But the aim of this broader definition of speech as writing is to flag this paradoxical nature. The ideal is an illusion, all language involves the risks Plato describes, which could never be expunged.

Language and communication are an inherently risky business.

Derrida introduces this notion of a 'general' or 'generalized' writing partly to question occasions when literal writing is devalued. In Derrida's 1972 work, *Dissemination* he discusses Plato's devaluation of writing insofar as it weakens memory and the assertion that 'live' spontaneous knowing seems to be threatened by written versions of knowledge. Plato claims that if we are just repeating at rote what we know because it is written down, or just because we recall it, we may not really know what we repeat. In this case, it is the phantom ideal of 'really knowing' which Plato considers under threat. The spectre of merely recalling, saying back to oneself, reiterating in one's mind what one knows, is here termed the 'general writing' where rote learning is at a kind of mental lag or remove from knowledge, as when I am just reproducing facts rather than 'actively' knowing them.

It isn't hard to lose confidence in the spontaneity or originality of our thought. Can I be sure I am not reproducing a thought I have merely acquired? Although it seems we think a thought at a precise moment, just one moment later my active thought seems to pass into the domain of memory, apparently a kind of mental record or reproduction of my thoughts. True instantaneity is a most evanescent phenomenon. Plato does not claim that only a true instantaneity is a real knowledge. But his work is full of debasing accounts of what seems to impede such knowledge, such as his devaluation of those who rely on written texts, and on rote memory.

Plato's debasement of writing implies his idealization of a thoroughly spontaneous, immediate, undeferred, therefore non-'inscribed' knowledge, or, thought. Derrida exposes this ideal as an impossible phantasy. In its ideal version, it would not be inscribed in sound, or air, or time. It would not be like writing at all. For Plato's abasement of writing to be coherent, there needs to be a contrasting possibility of purity. Arguing that the pure version of language is in fact impossible, Derrida shows that the devaluation is therefore invalid, depicting a kind of virus that has already infected whatever this purity is supposed to be 'from the inside'. In Derrida's view, the traditional, implicit ideal was never pure. Spectres of impurity serve only to sustain the phantom promise of the ideal.

Although consciousness is considered the origin of both speech and writing, Plato does not seat the origin of conscious knowledge in humans. Instead, our thought is a kind of mental image of the 'ideal' forms that Plato considered the true origin of the human world. Just as he considered worldly wooden chairs to be copies of a pure, ideal form of a chair, human knowledge was a kind of copy or approximation of original ideas, the true origin of the world.

According to Derrida, the 'virus' of secondary (the possibility of copies, of knowledge and language) had crept even into this ideal of origin. He argues that 'immortality and perfection . . . would consist in having no relation at all with any outside' (Derrida 1981A, 101). When reading Plato deconstructively, Derrida finds evidence that Plato's ideal forms always have a relation with the human world. For Plato, ideal forms are copied in the world and approximately understood with human language. Derrida suggests that their very 'copiability' by language is a kind of contamination by the exterior virus. The ideal '*adds to itself* the possibility of being *repeated* as such' (Derrida 1981A, 168).

Derrida argues that language always involves delay, deferral of meaning, ambiguity, some degree of the speaker's 'distance', the possibility of confusion, deception and unreliability, all factors that Plato considers negative. Rather than lamenting or condemning these facets of language, or considering them somehow avoidable, Derrida regards them as integral to it. Without the play of these elements, there would be no language. By definition, language is always somehow escaping us. Under the expanded deconstructive definition, all language is a 'form of writing'.

# 2

# READING AS INTERVENTION

Though the 'non-mastery ... of an appropriated language' ... qualifies, above all, more literally and more sensitively, some situations of 'colonial' alienation or historical servitude, this definition, so long as it is imprinted with the requisite inflections, also carries well beyond these determinate conditions. It also holds for what would be called the language of the master, the *hospes*, or the colonist.

Quite far from dissolving the always relative specificity, however cruel, of situations of linguistic oppression or colonial expropriation, this prudent and differentiated universalization must account, and I would even say that it is the only way one can account, for the *determinable* possibility of a subservience and a hegemony. And even account for a terror inside languages (inside languages there is a terror, soft, discreet, or glaring; that is our subject). For contrary to what one is often most tempted to believe, the master is nothing. And he does not have exclusive possession of anything. Because the master does not possess exclusively, and *naturally*, what he calls his lan-

guage, because, whatever he wants or does, he cannot
maintain any relations of property or identity that are natural, national, congenital, or ontological, with it, because
he can give substance to and articulate [*dire*] this appropriation only in the course of an unnatural process of
politico-phantasmatic constructions, because language is
not his natural possession he can, thanks to that very fact,
pretend historically, through the rape of a cultural usurpa-
tion, which means always essentially colonial, to
appropriate it in order to impose it as 'his own'. That is his
belief: he wishes to make others share it through the use of
force or cunning.

Extract from Derrida 1998A, 23

The American analytic philosopher John Searle once scath-
ingly agreed with Derrida that one could plausibly argue that
speech is writing. One only need redefine writing in terms
broad enough that they will include speech also. One could
argue that white is black, if one defined the gradations of
blackness broadly enough as to include the extreme of white
on its broad spectrum. Deconstruction was, in Searle's opinion
not false, but trivial: 'by such methods, one can prove anything.
One can prove that the rich are really poor, the true is really
false, etc.' (Searle 1983, 76–7). Why would one take the trouble
to do so, or to question the tautology that white is white?

An answer emerges when we consider the way people's
sense of identity can often be an aspiration to identity. In a
racial context the statement 'white is white' is anything but
tautological. The statement might be uttered as a declaration
of a racist passion, a call to upholding exclusion, the ideology
that white *should* be white, the anxiety that white *might not* be
white, the threat that whiteness might be endangered, the

covert avowal that whiteness is not as self-evident as it pretends and declares. In such contexts, violence is literally at work in the declaration that white is white. There's nothing trivial about the deconstructibility of this declaration and the related aspiration to racial purity. Derrida provokes us to read deconstructively in contexts of aspiration and denigration, of idealization and debasement, of protection and exclusion. His early claims that philosophical discussions of language were such a context made him a controversial intellectual at least in philosophical circles. Though he never repudiated these claims, later work addressing state policies, race, nation, culture and democracy has been less contentious as the implications of his philosophical discussions have emerged. The extract opening this chapter, from Derrida's *Monolinguism of the Other*, dates from this later period. It was written two decades after the excerpt from *Dissemination* discussed in chapter one.

*Monolinguism of the Other* challenges the belief in cultural or linguistic authenticity. Derrida claims that notions of one's proper home and one's proper language are always problematic (Derrida 1998A, 59–60) and their consequences can be cruel. Because of a country's pretension to natural or historical entitlement, many immigrants find themselves denied residence in countries where they seek entry or asylum. Derrida challenges the hierarchical opposition between the entitled and the unentitled, and between the colonizer and the colonized.

A colonized people undergoes land loss and the imposition of the colonizer's culture and law. Some might like to believe they have not been colonized, and are not exposed to the threat of colonization. Derrida intervenes, suggesting that if we think of colonization in a sufficiently broad way, we could all be described as colonized. He defines culture itself as a kind of colonization. As children, we all are introduced into cultures, territories, laws and identities which we eventually identify as 'ours'. We find ourselves born in a nation, implicated in its history, and immersed in the language that we acquire. Law, land and language do not properly belong even to those who are legally 'British', 'American' or 'Australian'. Both legal and natural born residents must acquire a language and culture. That acquisition is less secure than we like to think. No one speaks their own language perfectly. Moreover, language is always in transition, involving a perpetual redefinition by experts and non-experts alike of its proper usage. The understanding of cultural identity is also in constant flux. Think of how in the late twentieth century 'multiculturalism' newly came to seem essentially 'British'. Legal entitlement to one's country is also less secure than some like to pretend. No one is entirely immune from the threat of losing their citizenship or homeland. A country may be invaded; or authorities may decide to disenfranchise certain of its citizens and have the power to do so; or a country may fragment into new nation states; or one may be driven away from one's country by the extremes of war, chaos or persecution.

It is possible to argue that we are all in some way unstable in our possession of culture and citizenship, colonized and vulnerable to further colonization, without arguing that we are all 'the same'. Instead, one can stress all the ways in which individuals and peoples are differently colonized. The point is not to deny the differences between colonizers and colonized peoples. Yet Derrida is hesitant about those who self-identify as having suffered cultural alienation and loss, if this takes the route of reinforcing the illusion that some are not alienated, and have a particularly legitimate relationship to their language and culture. Derrida's point is that no one has a thoroughly legitimate relationship to language and culture. To this end, he questions the self-created privilege of the nativist or colonizer who pretends to a natural or historical right to exclude others. In *Monolinguism of the Other*, he argues that anyone claiming the right to deprive others of land or admission to a country, or the right to set conditions for inclusion, disavows the instability of his or her own entitlement. Therefore, he says of colonialization and linguistic disappropriation:

> This exceptional situation is, at the same time, certainly exemplary of a universal structure; it represents or reflects a type of original 'alienation' that institutes every language as a language of the other: the impossible property of language. But that must not lead to a kind of neutralization of differences. (Derrida 1998A, 63)

One can argue that we are all colonized and alienated, without claiming that we are all colonized and alienated in the same way.

Derrida terms this 'general' colonialism, in the same way he considers a 'general' toxic body, a 'general' unnatural maternity, a general vulnerability to terrorism, and a 'general' writing. In making this point, Derrida's aim is not to level all differences, but to challenge self-created authority, in this case cultural authority. Some do consider their language their own. Some believe they can impose on immigrants the duty to learn the language and customs of their new country. This assumes those already occupying it have a 'proper' relationship to their culture and their mother tongue and are fully adapted to it, disavowing the fact that no one has a perfect command of language or culture, nor is fully adapted to their country, nor is a country one simple, self-identical entity to which one could be fully adapted. The depiction of the colonized and immigrants as somehow linguistically and culturally 'improper' reinforces a false mystique: that the natural born and naturalized are thoroughly at home in their language and at one with their culture. Deconstruction asks certain kinds of questions, and not others. This makes it a tool to be drawn upon, rather than a philosophical system. It does not ask the question: should immigrants be expected to learn the language and customs of a new country? It does ask the question: how can we turn such expectations into a critique of the 'legitimate' citizen's idealizing and self-serving self-understanding?

Deconstruction can prompt changes in perceptions in politics and culture. It calls for a critique of ideas sometimes taken for granted: in this case, that some are at home in their language and culture, and entitled to their country, as 'foreigners' are not. These suppositions are to be resisted because inclusion occurs at the price of exclusion, and the legitimacy of the latter is falsely asserted. Some countries, governments, groups and individuals will engage in practices of exclusion. But it is one thing to negotiate directly, and as responsibly as possible, with the dilemmas arising from excluding others in the *absence* of one's own natural entitlement. It is another to pretend, deceptively, to natural entitlement.

Derrida asserts, in a well-known comment, that 'deconstruction is *not neutral* . . . It *intervenes*' (Derrida 1981C, 93). He has been involved in a number of political activities. As a member of the International Parliament of Writers, he supported the proposal for cities of refuge for persecuted intellectuals. He joined public calls for peace in Algeria and Palestine, was a frequent presence in French newspapers

commenting critically on public affairs, protested at the death
sentence of incarcerated African-American journalist Mumia
Abu-Jamal, and critiqued the harsh immigration policy in
France. Yet he does not have a programme for action or
activism. When he claims that deconstruction intervenes, his
political activities are not what he has in mind. Instead,
Derrida provokes us to read differently: with a closer attention
to instability, contradiction, the unstable forces of idealization
and debasement. He asks us, how can we read differently, for
example, the claims of some to natural authority, ownership
and privilege? He prompts us to think in new ways and more
critically about received ideas and arguments whether they
belong to politics, history, philosophy or contemporary
culture.

Derrida proposes that we rethink the ideal of cultural unity
through the generalization of a concept of cultural and individual disunity. This means not just that different cultures exist
side by side, but that each of those entities we think of as a
'different culture' is internally plural and fractured, itself composed of conflicting elements. It is not sufficient to say of
Britain or France that they are composed of many communities if this wrongly suggests that each of those communities is
homogeneous. What if we said that each of those communities is composed of many different individuals? Even so, we
might be suggesting that each individual is a simplistic thing.
A nation does not consist in those who share the same beliefs.
Neither do the communities composing it. Nor even do the
individuals composing those communities. An individual can
be composed of many conflicting beliefs and interests, like a
community and a nation. This, in Derrida's view, is no bad
thing. He claims that a state in which there was only unity or
oneness would be 'a terrible catastrophe', 'not even . . . a

state'. Plurality and respect for plurality are vital to states: 'Thus, a state as such must be attentive as much as possible to plurality, to the plurality of peoples, of languages, cultures, ethnic groups, persons, and so on' (Derrida 1997A, 15). However, when pluralism is espoused as a value, it is often through the attribution of an individual and characteristic identity to a language, culture or ethnic group. Derrida's approach is distinctive for its alternative attempt to think of plurality as a value without attributing individual identity to the persons and groups of which plurality is constituted: 'the people who fight for their identity must pay attention to the fact that identity . . . implies a difference within identity'.

Derrida thinks that deconstruction can prompt new ways of thinking about cultural and individual identity: 'Once you take into account this inner and other difference, then you pay attention to the other and you understand that fighting for your own identity is not exclusive of another identity, is open to another identity' (Derrida 1997A, 13). In Derrida's view, there are not just differences between self-identical people. There are also differences within people. 'I' am fractured. For example, 'I' am fractured by my differentiation from others. Take a domestic example, for instance my relation with my sister. Imagine I tell you that we are very different. In that case, it may seem – at least to me – that I am my own person, so is my sister, and that differences lie between us. Derrida would disagree, suggesting that part of my identity – part of the 'I' in question *is* my differentiation from (and relation to) my sister. That difference and relationality constitutes my identity. We would make a mistake, then, in thinking of plu- rality as a matter of one plus one plus one. We need to rethink how each of those individual elements is constituted through its fracturing by relationality and differentiation. Relations between peoples, cultures and communities must be thought along similar lines.

A culture gains its self-definition through its differentiation from and relation to other peoples. Could recognition of this point involve a better relationship with other peoples? Occasionally Derrida's tone is optimistic, as in the comment: 'once you take into account this inner . . . difference, then you pay attention to the other' (Derrida 1997A, 13). Such a viewpoint 'prevents totalitarianism, nationalism, egocentrism, and so on' (Derrida 1997A, 13–14). Often, cultural disunity is thought of as precluding cultural harmony. Derrida suggests the inverse approach. Perhaps it is the idealization of an impossibly cultural unity and harmony that leads to the devaluation of cultural disunity. Perhaps if we valued cultural disunity more, we would be less authoritarian, and deprecating of difference. He is not proposing a recipe for cultural progress, but asking us to rethink the supposition that disunity is responsible for violent totalitarianism and nationalism. It may be the opposite. It may be the elevation of impossible ideals of cultural identity that is responsible. Think of how immigration has recently been held responsible for increased racial violence in Britain. Is this true, or is it the authoritarian idealizing of cultural identity by all concerned that is partly responsible?

A deconstructive reading intervenes in several ways. It offers new techniques for identifying contradictions in politics so that we gain a heightened awareness to particular forms of inconsistency (for example, in the representations of the identity of a nation or community or of its legitimacy). Exposing these can be a useful critical tool when it is a matter of resisting exclusions. Second, a successful deconstruction *changes* a text. It renders it more foreign, or alien to us. This can be positive when a text promotes a tradition, message or political platform we know all too well. Deconstruction offers a means of changing our understanding of the ideas we inherit from the past and by which we are affected and effected in the present. Third, a deconstructive reading offers new ways of conceiving the onus of responsibility. If we are dazzled less by impossible ideals – of democracy, justice, nature, cultural origin, even a pure understanding or a fully harmonious community – we begin to formulate new forms of ethics and politics. Fourth, we will see that in his middle to late work, Derrida stresses that texts, contexts and traditions open themselves up to new possibilities for transformation through their relationship with 'impossibility'.

In *Positions* (1972), Derrida defines deconstruction as a way of dislodging hierarchical oppositions governed by idealization and debasement:

> a kind of *general strategy of deconstruction* . . . is to avoid both simply *neutralizing* the binary oppositions of metaphysics and simply *residing* within the closed field of these oppositions, thereby confirming it. Therefore we must proceed using a double gesture . . . On the one hand, we must traverse a phase of *overturning*. To do justice to this necessity is to recognize that in a classical philosophical opposition we are not dealing with the peaceful co-existence of a *vis-à-vis*, but rather with a violent hierarchy. One of the two terms governs the other (axiologically, logically, etc.), or has the upper hand. To deconstruct the opposition, first of all, is to overturn the hierarchy at a given moment. To overlook this phase of overturning is to forget the conflictual and subordinating structure of opposition. Therefore one might proceed too quickly to a *neutralization*

that *in practice* would leave the previous field untouched, leaving one no hold on the previous opposition, thereby preventing any means of *intervening* in the field effectively ... That being said – and on the other hand – to remain in this phase is still to operate on the terrain of and from within the deconstructed system. By means of this double, and precisely stratified, dislodged and dislodging, writing, we must also mark the interval between inversion, which brings low what was high, and the irruptive emergence of a new 'concept', a concept that can no longer be, and never could be, included in the previous regime. (Derrida 1981C, 41–2)

Derrida targets notions of 'fall' and 'origin' (Derrida 1981C, 53). Whatever the context, the debasing of 'x' can be a means of elevating the image of 'y', in the name of an ideal 'z'. A deconstructive reading will identify 'z' as having always been contaminated in some way by what is attributed to 'x'. Derrida proposes that the ideal is impossible. Therefore, the elevated cosmetic image of 'y' is illegitimate. The primacy of speech over writing in Plato's dialogues may seem innocuous but the deconstruction of origin when applied to other contexts and disciplines often has clearer social and political implications. Identities, ideals and valued points of reference are often illegitimately maintained through debasement.

In historical contexts of race hierarchy, idealized whiteness was distanced from what was thought to contaminate it. In the nineteenth century, white Europeans nourished their self-image through juxtaposition with the uncivilized, native other, for example, as in depictions of Africa and India during the era of European colonialism. Derrida considers such debasement as violent, a term meant literally, as in Derrida's deconstructive essays on the apartheid regime in South Africa. It can also be understood in a broader sense, as when Derrida exposes illegitimate arrogation of authority as a kind of violence.

Derrida describes his 'reading' as an 'overturning' of a hierarchy. Whether his context is anthropology, philosophy of mind or language, ancient philosophy, psychoanalysis, biology, genetics, politics, public policy or sexuality, Derrida discusses instances when there is idealization of the pure, the natural or the original, and devaluation of what is considered unnatural, impure or 'fallen'. He suggests that such devaluations give more cosmetic stability or identity to what is valued. Such a reading overturns these hierarchies suggesting ways in which the devaluation has the 'upper hand' over what is valued. It would have been more difficult to assert white superiority in colonial politics without its deprecation of and contrast to its negative opposite: the image of the savage, barbaric other. Pointing out this dependency on the 'other' is a means of reversing the hierarchy. Rather than the colonized depending on the British colonizer for exposure to civilization, it is the latter who depends on a stereotyped image of the native for an enhanced self-depiction as 'civilized'.

# 3

# DIFFÉRANCE

The writer writes *in* a language and *in* a logic whose proper system, laws and life his discourse by definition cannot dominate absolutely. He uses them only by letting himself, after a fashion and up to a point, be governed by the system. And the reading must always aim at a certain relationship, unperceived by the writer, between what he commands and what he does not command of the patterns of language that he uses . . . a signifying structure that critical reading should *produce*.

What does produce mean here? In my attempt to explain that, I would initiate a justification of my principles of reading . . .

To produce this signifying structure obviously cannot consist of reproducing, by the effaced and respectful doubling of commentary, the conscious, voluntary, intentional relationship that the writer institutes [though] . . . without this recognition and respect, critical production would risk developing in any direction at all and authorize itself to say almost anything. But this indispensable guardrail has always only *protected*, it has never *opened*, a reading.

> Yet if reading must not be content with doubling the text, it cannot legitimately transgress the text toward something other than it, toward a referent (a reality that is metaphysical, historical, psychobiographical, etc.) or toward a signified outside the text whose content could take place, could have taken place outside of language . . . *There is nothing outside of the text* [there is no outside-text; *il n'y a pas de hors-texte*].
>
> Extract from Derrida 1997B, 157–8

In *Of Grammatology*, his first major work, Derrida presents deconstruction as a critical reading of texts which brings to light what is already at work in the texts he deconstructs. But through his intervention we see the text differently. He discusses the frequently conflicting relationship between an author's expressed intentions – or the 'declared' level of the text – and what the text actually 'describes' (demonstrates or does). He pays attention to ambivalent ideas within a text which are inconsistent with its overt statements. For that reason, deconstruction is not mere commentary, redoubling or reproduction. The text's 'declarations' are its own account of what it considers high and low, original and degraded. Deconstruction brings to light suppressed textual conflicts concerning what is ideal, primary or original and what is degradation or insufficiency. To overtly juxtapose a text's declared and described levels is to produce a different text.

*Of Grammatology* is a work that spans several different disciplines: linguistics, anthropology, and the history of philosophy, and includes transformative readings of Rousseau, the turn-of-the-century linguist Ferdinand de Saussure, and the twentieth-century anthropologist Claude Lévi-Strauss. These writers belong to different disciplines, and to different historical periods. As a result, *Of Grammatology* seems an eclectic, fragmented, multi-disciplinary work, but its themes interrelate. Derrida focuses on the hierarchies between speech and writing; and nature and culture in these different writers. He asks how we should read these hierarchies. We have already seen that early work by Derrida also requires us to come to terms with the classical texts he is reading: confronting not just Derrida, but Derrida and Plato, for example. Similarly, an important Derridean term, *différance*, arises from his appropriation of Saussure's concept of the 'sign'. In addition to his strategy of reversal, Derrida finds or invents new concepts that can't be contained within overturned hierarchical oppositions. *Différance* is one of these terms. In relation to the opposition between 'presence' and 'absence' *différance* is neither present, nor absent. Instead, it is a kind of absence that generates the effect of presence. It is neither identity, nor difference. Instead, it is a kind of differentiation that produces the effect of identity and of difference between those identities.

In his *Course in General Linguistics*, Saussure observed the way a language was a system of elements he termed signs. The meaning of each sign appears to be 'present'; in fact it is not. He argued that meaning was produced through the relationship between signs. A sign – 'dog' – may seem to represent an animate being, a four-legged animal now running in my backyard. But if we consult its meaning in the dictionary, we will be directed to other meanings, and from those we will be similarly re-directed. My dictionary tells me that a dog is a quadruped of many breeds, wild and domesticated. It thereby defers the definition, directing me to further consult the meanings for quadruped, breed, wild and domesticated. Their definitions would in turn require others. Moreover, my dictionary tells me of many ideas with which the dog is associated: the worthless or surly person, astronomical constellations; it gives me a list of colloquial expressions such as 'every dog will have its day'; it reminds me of dogs in mangers, dogs in blankets, dogfish and dog-faced baboons. The meaning of the dog is suspended differentially across such associations, and never quite settles.

Meaning, Saussure concluded, is never fully, or finally, present. For this reason, he argued that with signs, 'we discover not *ideas* given in advance but *values* emanating from the [linguistic] system . . . [T]hese concepts are purely differential, not positively defined by their content but negatively defined by their relations with other terms of the system. Their most precise characteristic is that they are what the others are not' (Saussure 1974, 117). Saussure's *Course* was extremely influential in many areas of French thought – among them psychoanalysis, anthropology and film theory.

Reiterating Saussure's theory, Derrida commented that 'the first consequence to be drawn from this is that the signified concept is never present in and of itself, in a sufficient presence that would refer only to itself . . . every concept is inscribed in a chain or in a system within which it refers to the other, to other concepts, by means of the systematic play of differences' (Derrida 1982A, 11). Derrida elaborates that the meaning of any apparently 'present' sign is nothing but the relationship between all the absent meanings that the term is not. The play of relational, differentiating linguistic value between all the absent terms is at work in any sign whose meaning we seem able to isolate. A sign is not autonomous of the network of alternative and combinatory elements from which it is derived. It is a false abstraction to lift a term 'dog' out of that system, and think that its meaning can be dissociated from the latter.

Instead, the meaning of dog is a relational play with many absent possibilities that 'ghost' the meaning in question. The meaning of the dog is an endless play between associated alternatives. What is a dog? It is 'not' exactly some other dog-ideas it might have been – hound, puppy or cur. Not exactly other sounds it might have been – a 'hog' or 'log'. Not exactly other pets it might have been – a cat or a bird. It is not exactly other non-literal usages it might have been – the hangover cure, the sleeping trouble we choose to ignore. Its meaning is produced through an infinite differentiation from possible alternatives. Derrida agrees that the meaning of the sign 'dog' is never definitively present. Instead its meaning arises in the connections between the associations and imagined substitutions of countless kinds – that is, sounds, different pets, breeds, metaphors.

In general, difference is often conceived as the difference between two purported identities: black and white, east and west, good and bad, man and woman, etc. In common speech, we refer to the 'difference between' this and that. Derrida invents the term *différance* to refer to the alternative understanding of difference just discussed: not the difference 'between' terms, but the passage of infinite, endless differentiation giving rise to apparent identities between which one might then argue there is difference.

'*Différance*' (from the verb différer, meaning both to differ and to defer) is a Derridean neologism referring to a differentiation which he also terms 'spacing', and which prevents any sign from having a self-enclosed identity. *Différance* is the unresolved deferral of the identity one might have ascribed to a particular term: an entirely fixed meaning for dog never definitively arrives. Meaning endlessly 'differs', and any original presence of meaning is endlessly 'deferred'.

Although it was developed from an amplified Saussurean theory, the Derridean term '*différance*' played a role in his deconstruction of Saussure's own work. Even in the work of Saussure, the hierarchy of speech over writing reoccurs. He devalues writing as a sign system whose sole purpose is to represent speech, arguing that the proper study of linguistics ought to focus on spoken forms of language. He considered writing an 'unnatural' linguistic object because it is merely the 'figuration' of speech.

The pejorative use of 'unnatural' to devalue writing is surprising, since Saussure argued of spoken signs that there was a 'non-natural' connection between signified content (concepts, such as the idea of a dog) and their signifiers (acoustic sound images, such as the sounds d-o-g). Insofar as the signifier and signified form that unity called a sign, Saussure argued, they have an 'arbitrary' relationship. He meant by this that there is no natural unity between d-o-g and the concept dog.

Derrida questions Saussure's devaluation of written signs as mere 'signs of signs' (signs of acoustic signs). Through a deconstructive reading he expands and generalizes the category we could refer to as 'signs of signs': 'Writing is not a sign of a sign, except if one says it of all signs, which would be more profoundly true. If every sign refers to a sign, and if "sign of a sign" signifies writing, certain conclusions – which I shall consider at the appropriate moment – will become inevitable' (Derrida 1997B, 43). Derrida rightly points out that although Saussure, to describe writing, uses the notion of 'sign of a sign' in a literal and pejorative sense (he probably means 'mere secondary copy'), Saussure has effectively also offered a much more broad and generalizing definition of signs as always signs of signs of signs of signs. Derrida argues that if Saussure so defines literal writing, all signs could be considered a generalized form of writing.

Texts – including Saussure's *Course*, a posthumously published reconstruction of his lectures – are often riddled with unstable hierarchies effecting fictions of presence, originality or naturality, as when Saussure associates the spoken with what is 'natural' in linguistics. Unexpectedly, given his view that their effects of presence arise from infinite differentiation, even Saussure had suggested spoken signs were original. Derrida points out the inconsistencies of this argument and suggests that it deconstructs itself.

Derrida's emphasis that every sign leads to a sign permits him to conclude, in the passage above with the famous statement that 'there is no outside of the text'. Derrida does not mean there is nothing in the world but ink on the page. The term 'text' in his work does not refer only to books, nor to literal writing on paper. Like the term 'writing' in his work, 'text' has been redefined by Derrida as the infinitely deferring movement of differentiation. He generalizes the term, and he suggests the alternative definition of 'text': a heterogeneous, differential and open field of forces (Derrida 1986A, 167–8).

The sentence 'there is nothing outside of the text' is not a statement about what there is, or is not in the world. The latter presupposes the category 'world', and the question 'what is true of that world?' It supposes that the 'world' comes first, as the origin of the secondary, descriptive sentences we generate about it and as guarantor of their truth or falsity. Unlike the traditional questions asked in philosophy, Derrida switches his philosophical game. Rather than asking 'what is there?', Derrida interrogates the tangles in which we become entwined when we ask what there is. We tend to project something original, which is subsequently known, represented or hypothesized by us. Origins, as we depict them, are always already enmeshed in language. They are relational (that is to say, they are depicted in relation with what supposedly comes after them, or represents them, or approximates them), and they are rhetorically rendered. In other words, our way of talking about origins, and about what is secondary to them, produces the 'effect' that there seems to be an origin. Like the sign 'dog', 'origin' is the effect of the movement of *différance*, of deferred and 'differentiated' meaning: the plays of language that project their supposedly original moment. Derrida could be considered indifferent to the question of 'what is there' in favour of 'how do we depict what there is?' For Derrida, origins are always depicted textually. Even to say that Derrida 'reserves his judgement' about what there 'is' collapses somewhat into what he avoids. It involves a sly suggestion that there may or may not be a 'beyond' to the plays of language about which he reserves his judgement. This is the beginning of a wordplay in which the 'world' and 'descriptive language' are already being figured in terms of oppositions between origin and secondarity.

Against the statement 'there is nothing outside of the text', critics erroneously respond: surely there is *something* outside of the text: atoms, blood, rain, trees, bodies? Derrida seems to deny 'reality' in favour of 'words'. This response misunderstands the sense in which Derrida means 'text'. Like writing, he widens its definition. 'Text' for Derrida is such things as *différance*, spacing, relationality, differentiation, deferral, delay. To say there is nothing outside the text is to say that there is always relationality and differentiation. No matter what we imagine as 'reality', it could be argued that differentiation is critical to it.

Consider each domain someone might select to refute the

claim that there is nothing outside of the text. The critic might object to Derrida: you say there is nothing outside of the text: but what of my current emotion of anger? That isn't a 'text'. The debate can't progress unless the critic recognizes what Derrida means by text. Some defend Derrida by pointing out that it is impossible to describe that anger without metaphors, linguistic meanings – we have always entered the world of language, thus the anger is not outside of textuality. Others would argue that the experience of emotion is already 'differential' (hate differentiates itself from disliking, love, etc.).

Similarly, some have tried to refute Derrida by mentioning the concrete materiality of a virus. One form of counter-argument points out how the scientific language of the virus is in fact highly metaphorical: viral attacks are often described with militaristic or battle imagery. This interpretation of Derrida emphasizes that we are always in the world of language, whether we refer to a virus, an emotion, the sun, the rain. We've never stepped out of language to touch the thing itself, according to this defence of Derrida. Even as the rain touches my face, it does so *with* associations and differentiations. It is the breaking of the drought, or the disaster to my clothes, or the joy of a sensation, or a marvellous memory rekindled. The rain does not fall without already being imbued with meaning for me. It cannot fall for me 'meaninglessly'.

However, such an explanation can tend to foster the mistaken – according to Derrida – suggestion that there is some kind of 'rain' in itself that I am, however, unable to experience except in the world of language and meaning. This too remains a deconstructible way of talking. It projects an 'original' world we believe we cannot access, trapped as we are in some prison of language.

What kind of material world might appear to be called into question by Derrida's claim that that there is nothing outside the text? Atoms, cells, chemicals, DNA, neuronal firing? Deconstructive writers on science such as Christopher Norris, Christopher Johnson and Elizabeth Wilson point out that we are not far from Derrida's definition of 'text'. The interconnections of atoms, or cells, or chemicals, or gene coding involve systems in which relational differences circulate whose spatiality and temporality, the spacing and connections and breaches between combinations and substitutions amount to energy, life, species, materiality, disposition, emotion. Johnson shows the parallel between Derrida's point that 'once inserted into another network the "same" philosopheme is no longer the same' (Derrida 1981B, 3) and the operation of genetic material: 'in genetic technology, alterations in the DNA of a cell are obtained by means of the splicing and grafting of sequences of the genetic code, and this recombination of sequences can serve to modify aspects of metabolism or anatomical structure' (Johnson 1993, 182). Rather than denying materiality, Derrida's argument that there is nothing outside the text stresses the importance of *différance* to materiality.

## 4

## UNDECIDABLES

The concept of the supplement . . . harbours within it two significations whose cohabitation is as strange as it is necessary. The supplement adds to itself, it is a surplus, a plenitude enriching another plenitude, the *fullest measure* of presence. It cumulates and accumulates presence. It is thus that art, *technè*, image, representation, convention, etc., come as supplements to nature and are rich with this entire cumulating function. This kind of supplementarity determines in a certain way all the conceptual oppositions within which Rousseau inscribes the notion of Nature to the extent that it *should* be self-sufficient.

But the supplement supplements. It adds only to replace. It intervenes or insinuates *in-the-place-of*; if it fills, it is as if one fills a void. If it represents and makes an image, it is by the anterior default of a presence. Compensatory [*suppléant*] and vicarious, the supplement is an adjunct, a subaltern instance which *takes-(the)-place* [*tient-lieu*]. As substitute, it is not simply added to the positivity of a presence, it produces no relief, its place is assigned in the structure by the mark of an emptiness.

> Somewhere, something can be filled up *of itself*, can
> accomplish itself, only by allowing itself to be filled
> through sign and proxy.
>
> Extract from Derrida 1997B, 144–5

In *Of Grammatology* Derrida argues that the term 'supplement'
as it is used by the eighteenth-century French philosopher
Jean-Jacques Rousseau is 'undecidable'. An undecidable is a
term, found or invented by Derrida, that does not fit com-
fortably into either of the two poles of a binary opposition.
Just as *différance* is neither 'presence' nor 'absence'; neither
'identity' nor 'difference', supplement is neither plenitude nor
deficiency. A common example of this undecidability
between plenitude and lack is to be found in the supplement
to an encyclopedia. The supplement has the connotation of
plenitude. In completing a deficiency, its purpose is to make
the encyclopedia complete. But in so doing, it also reconfig-
ures the encyclopedia as having been deficient, because, if not
for the supplement, it would have had the status of being
complete. In this sense, the supplement has the connotations
of both 'plenitude' and 'lack' and is 'undecidable'. It makes
something deficient in the same moment as it completes it. Its
meaning is neither the one term – plenitude – nor the other
term – lack. It is, as Derrida likes to say of undecidables, both
and neither.

*Of Grammatology* discusses the supplementarity of nature as
an undecidable in the work of Rousseau. Derrida demonstrates that many hierarchical and binary oppositions circulate
throughout Rousseau's literary, philosophical, autobiographical and political works. These include origin versus fall, high
versus low, purity versus degradation, virtue versus corrup-
tion. These oppositions intersect with a dominant hierarchy

between nature and culture. Rousseau often depicts a state of nature in which humans might hypothetically have existed, but 'nature' has many ramifications in his work. In his novel, *Julie, or the New Heloise* Rousseau depicts a small familial community organized according to nature's principles. His famous work on pedagogy, *Emile*, describes how young men and women can be raised following the dictates of nature. His political work *The Social Contract* offers a theory of the foundation of human political bonds. Given that these are artificial, Rousseau asks how we got from a state of nature to a sophisticated political organization relying on an implicit social pact.

In a transformative reading, Derrida refigures Rousseau's main concerns. If his intervention is successful, we will be persuaded that Derrida pinpoints Rousseau's preoccupations accurately. Derrida argues that Rousseau is preoccupied with the problem of supplementarity. Though sometimes, Derrida invents terms and concepts which are undecidable in order to disrupt hierarchical oppositions, just as often he will find these elements lurking in the texts he deconstructs. Whereas *différance* is an invented term, 'supplement' is one of these troubling and internally destabilizing, 'found' terms.

Throughout his writings, Rousseau describes everything romantic, sexual, sentimental, historic, formational, educational, political and cultural as a supplement. He describes masturbation as an unnatural supplement to reproductive sexuality. He also describes writing as a supplement to speech; evil as a supplement to nature; education as a supplement for natural deficiency; nurses as supplements to natural mothers; exploitation as a supplement to autonomy; mining as a supplement to nature; the women he loves as a supplement for his lost, loved mother; and new beloveds as supplements for women he has previously loved. Is the notion of the supplement coherent within his writings? To answer this question, we must ask: if everything is a supplement, what is supposed to 'have been' supplemented?

For Rousseau's ideal to be coherent, nature would have to be free of what he depicts as contamination, or degradation, or copy, or replacement. Instead, Derrida argues that Rousseau-ist purity and originality are not uncontaminated and that if the natural was thoroughly uncontaminated, there would be no possibility of its becoming unnatural. The *pharmakon* in Plato – another undecidable – and the supplement in Rousseau are represented by their authors as 'like an aggressor or a housebreaker, threatening some internal purity or security' (Derrida 1997B, 36). Derrida's countering suggestion is that the housebreaker lurks in the interior, waiting to open the door to a band of burglars.

In other words, Derrida suggests that the purported contamination or degradation is already enfolded inside. He suggests many spatial terms for this rhetorical phenomenon, including the *repli*: that which re-enfolds. He suggests that Rousseau introduces new divisions wherever he indulges in his ideals, folding over and reduplicating the nature/culture and purity/degradation oppositions. Instead of stable origins, Derrida argues that there are 'reflecting pools, and images' without a spring or a source: difference itself is the origin. 'For what is reflected is split *in itself*' (Derrida 1997B, 36).

Derrida's early description of deconstruction in *Positions*, extracted earlier, proposes that during deconstructive readings there is a phase of overturning an opposition, or bringing 'low' what was 'high'. He brings low the notion of plenitude, by pointing out that whatever is deemed plenitude is implicitly a kind of deficiency. He suggests that in Rousseau's work, where idealized women substitute for his lost mother, enfolded in the memory of the lost mother is an impossible feeling of plenitude, satisfaction or happiness Rousseau never had. He is never able to establish an original moment of nature that isn't also deemed a loss of some earlier moment. His depictions of natural states – historical or hypothetical – of the human are famously changeable. They include small agrarian communities, primitive humans with language, pre-linguistic primitive humans, early property owning communities and humans prior to the concept of property, primitive females prior and post to the genesis of pity, or the genesis of the family unit. Moreover, every supposedly original state contains the possibility of its own loss in the form of its immanent degradation or substitution, replacement or supplementation. The origin is not autonomous of the supplement. Derrida questions Rousseau's devaluation of some kinds of purportedly unnatural women and some social forms as unnatural where Rousseau is unable to give a coherent account of the natural.

Derrida's interest in supplementarity extends well beyond its use by Rousseau. Terms of privilege like 'speech' or 'white' or 'normal' are sometimes given positive connotations while nonetheless also falling short of some ideal. The origin is deferred, despite the devaluation of certain forms as inadequate to it. Derrida describes this spatial and temporal movement as 'deferral': where the original or ideal in question is never definitively pinpointed, always deferred. He notes a reiterating phenomenon where privileged terms are at once 'high' and 'low', 'good' and 'bad', whether the context is anthropology, ancient Greek philosophy, family values, or a politician's platform.

For example, in the current American climate, homosexuality and same-sex marriage are frequently denounced in the name of 'family values'. Heterosexuality is the ideal, deemed 'natural', yet those who condemn the unnatural in the name of heterosexuality tend not to be satisfied by heterosexuality alone. Heterosexuality must be 'really' heterosexual, and 'weak' versions (childless marriages, women who terminate pregnancies, women who work, men who do housework, liberal values, non-monogamy, heterosexuals engaging in sexual practices considered 'unnatural') cause unease amongst those whose mission is to promote family values, deemed original and natural. A satirical piece in the *New Yorker* presented the writer's ironic reasoning that even a constitutional reform banning same-sex marriages would not go far enough. It would still leave available the possibility of marriages between effeminate men and insufficiently feminine women. Joked the writer, isn't the phenomenon of 'samish sex marriage' also disturbingly unnatural? To arrive at the ideal of family values perhaps we should give points for sufficiently strong gender differentialism so that marriages ensured a conservative gender contrast between the partners (Saunders 2004). The wit nicely touches on a Derridean point.

In the conservative vision, there is displacement from one privileged term ('heterosexual'), to another ('conventional marriage'), to another (traditionally gendered men and women), to another ('sex differentiated, gender conservative, sexually traditional, conventional marriage). The unceasingly refined negotiation of what the conservative really privileges as 'natural' or 'biological' or 'virtuous' or 'intended by God', creates the illusion that these refinements are moving us closer to 'values', or morality, or God, or nature. Their definition is never complete and always in some sense deferred.

The conservative vision is characteristically troubled. Terms of privilege are both 'high' and 'low', both positive and negative. Like Rousseau's nature, heterosexuality is both 'good' and 'bad' – those who consider homosexuality unnatural are more than ready to denounce certain forms of heterosexuality as unnatural. New divisions arise with ever new projections of what is original, for the origin is already split within itself.

Terms deemed original have an intimate relationship with what is secondary to them or supplements them. What is the meaning of a God without human worshippers? What is the meaning of Platonic ideals except as the original of worldly copies? What is the meaning of the origin of the human as recounted by the Bible except as the capacity for that which is deemed sin and fall? Derrida suggests that this relationality with its supplement contaminates the supposed purity of any possible origin. Derrida appropriated the term 'supplement' which he uncovered in Rousseau and applied it to texts throughout his career.

When such pretensions to ideal origins are in play, a deconstructive reading may counter that origins are open to their 'outside'. This is the *repli*, or folding over of the exterior at the heart of the interior. Many depictions of the origin might be reinterpreted as describing that which is made deficient by the supplement, and thus are not 'self-present' or 'autonomous' but rather, in a relationship with that which copies, comes after them, or serves as their representation, expression, degradation or fall.

This is a good opportunity to reflect on what Derrida does when he reads. Derrida's description of Plato, Saussure and Rousseau in *Dissemination* and *Of Grammatology* is an intervention which brings to light rhetorical tendencies that might indicate ambivalences in a text. Through close attention we can locate refrains in their work which may be different to the common perception. With his characteristic style, Derrida ventriloquizes, or embodies with his own voice, the writing of Plato and Rousseau, all the while reconfiguring it. He brings to the fore obscured elements that may be overlooked or neglected by more conventional readings. When Derrida claims, in *Dissemination*, that writing must 'return to what it should have never ceased to be': accessory, accident and excess, his authorial voice can be confusing. In this case Derrida is 'reading' Plato. Derrida does not actually think that writing should 'return' to being an accident, though Derrida wrote this sentence. He is not repeating Plato either, because Plato's point is not that writing 'should' be devalued in order to 'restore the purity of the inside'. The argument belongs to Plato as transformed by Derrida. Derrida is 'voicing' Plato. When the deconstructive reading is successful, we are likely to read figures such as Plato, Rousseau and Saussure in new and different ways. We're more likely to be suspicious of devaluations of writing, to query the legitimacy or coherence of those devaluations and to think they may be sustained with a kind of illegitimate force or 'violence'.

# 5

## CULTURE, GENDER AND POLITICS

*What is proper to a culture is to not be identical to itself.*
Not to not have an identity, but not to be able to identify
itself, to be able to say 'me' or 'we'; to be able to take the
form of a subject only in the non-identity to itself or, if you
prefer, only in the difference *with itself* [*avec soi*]. There is
no culture or cultural identity without this difference *with
itself*. A strange and slightly violent syntax: 'with itself'
[*avec soi*] also means 'at home (with itself)' [*chez soi*]
(with, *avec*, is '*chez*', *apud hoc*). In this case, self-
difference, difference to itself [*difference à soi*], that which
differs and diverges from itself, of itself, would also be the
*difference (from) with itself* [*difference (d') avec soi*], a difference at once internal and irreducible to the 'at home
(with itself)' [*chez soi*]. It would gather and divide just as
irreducibly the center or hearth [*foyer*] of the 'at home (with
itself).' In truth it would gather this centre, relating
to itself, only to the extent that it would open up to this
divergence.

This can be said, inversely or reciprocally, of all identity
or all identification: there is no self-relation, no relationship
with oneself, without culture, but a culture of oneself *as* a
culture *of* the other, a culture of the double genitive and of

the *difference to oneself*. The grammar of the double genitive also signals that a culture never has a single origin.
Monogenealogy would always be a mystification in the history of culture.

Extract from Derrida 1992C, 9–11

Derrida is concerned that those who value ethnic origin or
purity may engage in 'appropriative madness' (Derrida
1998A, 24). He's generally wary of explaining the self, identity or experience by reference to one's historical or cultural
origins. This does not mean he believes one should avoid
historical or autobiographical self-reference. It's a matter of
whether one self-refers in a way that pretends one's origins are
fixed, or whether one interrogates their unstable and gaping
nature. In several autobiographical writings (such as
'Circumfession' (1993) and the discussions published as *Sur
Parole* (1999B)), he discusses his ambivalent relationship to
being French-Algerian and Jewish, which he terms Franco-
Maghrebian, in origin. Rather than projecting a personal
origin that is unified and fixable, Derrida stresses its divided
nature. He both rejects and identifies with metropolitan
France. He finds similar divisions in his relationship with academia, with his family origins, and his sexual identity.

In his discussion of European politics in *The Other Heading*
(1992C), he argues that one can't simply endorse a politics of
'difference' or 'specificity'. Europe would be propelled into a
fragmentation of 'self-enclosed idioms' and 'petty little nation-
alisms'. On the other hand, one can't endorse the traditional,
hegemonic authority of 'Europe'. How do we simultaneously
encompass *and* deconstruct both fragmentation and unifica-
tion, idealized specificities and hegemonic globalization, local
law and international law (Derrida 1995A, 360). Derrida

emphasizes that responsibility lies in negotiating contradiction without the promise of resolution. This political position tries to negotiate with and make visible the expense paid by an other, or the maintenance of hierarchical norms that accompany progress. Ongoing thoughtful negotiation is an improvement on authoritarian self-justification. Derrida's concept of responsibility arises in the absence of an umbrella of secured values or ideals. It does not affirm irresponsibility, and is not nihilism or quietism. Compare it to existentialism, for which a notion of freedom is affirmed in the absence of a horizon of reliable moral ideals. Derrida offers nothing so concrete. He articulates a burden that is placed on us, the responsibility with which we are left when we have no clearly defined concepts of responsibility except those deconstructible concepts we have inherited.

Derrida is a philosopher sensitive to difference in context, but he cautions those who engage in social activism – feminism, race or national or cultural politics – to be wary about so-called identity politics. We saw in chapter two the reservations he expresses about strategies of reversal which aim only to make high what was low; to raise the status of what has been devalued. His aim is to disrupt ideals of identity rather than fix them. He has commented, 'I resist this movement that tends towards a narcissism of minorities that is developing everywhere – including within feminist movements' (Derrida 2004, 21).

Though Derrida expresses ambivalence about some forms of feminism, a considerable amount of his work has been concerned with deconstructing the opposition between masculinity and femininity. From almost his earliest work, Derrida was interested in how sex, sexual difference, genealogy and women have figured in the history of philosophy, so

much so that *Of Grammatology* has been described as possess-
ing 'a strangely "feminist" voice' (Jardine 1985, 188). In some
early works, *différance* became the term for sexual differing and
deferring, and an endless play of sexual differentiation, that
would call into question sexual identity, and the certainty of
being a thoroughly male man or a thoroughly female woman.
Is anybody's maleness or femaleness definitive? It is a matter of
a complex network of meanings for biology, behaviour, sexuality, genealogy. Early in his work, we find Derrida playing
with this question and casting into doubt the consistency with
which he was, and wrote like, a man.

Feminists were divided in their response. Some saw considerable potential in a deconstructive feminism, while others
were caustic about Derrida, perceiving an appropriation of
feminist reflection. Moreover, in two controversial publications ('Women in the Beehive' 1987 and 'Choreographies'
1997) Derrida expresses doubts about the process of institu-
tionalizing feminism. Feminism might have to renounce its
confidence in progress (Derrida and McDonald 1997, 25)
and the supposition that history moves, all going well, from
a less feminist past to a more feminist future. Yet such
suggestions are combined with his affirmation of gender
studies and feminist goals. Several of Derrida's deconstructive
readings analyse the so-called phallocentrism of classical
philosophers, in the sense that a power, privilege and authority associated with masculinity has been rendered 'central'
or 'original', and femininity has historically been seen as inferior to, a derivation of, or secondary to masculinity. In this
respect, Derrida's project is of interest to feminist readers.
However, feminism may not be free of the idealization and
debasement he criticizes in the phallocentric tradition. To
extend Derrida's attunement to the possible presence of

debasement and idealization to feminism need not be seen as
anti-feminist.

The suggestion seems to be that any feminism should be
accompanied with a simultaneous effort to deconstruct feminism. This can be a constructive contribution to feminism.
Many feminist writers have engaged in self-criticism about
feminism's failure to adequately include the perspectives and
priorities of women from different backgrounds, classes and
cultures. Feminism itself has had origins in overly homoge-
nous notions of the rights entitled to the female subject
(frequently imagined as white and middle class). At the
extreme, feminist struggles for sex equality have been accompanied by notions of class or race hierarchy.

For example, when nineteenth-century feminists made the
case for women's right to education and enfranchisement, it
was common to juxtapose this possibility with the spectre of
the savage and primitive from which women were to be elevated. At one end of the spectrum lay the spectre of the
primitive, at the other the beacon of the enfranchised, well-
educated woman with legal and property rights. A Derridean
reading heightens one's sensitivity to the interwined process of
idealization and abasement that was, historically, at work in
feminism's hopes. We shouldn't be surprised that the 'poor',
the 'primitive', the 'uneducated' are imagined as the shame-
ful face that feminism wishes to go beyond. Derrida has
repeatedly argued that it is impossible not to believe in and
hope for progress. Nevertheless, one should also be attuned to
what or who pays the price for one's on-going ideals.

Feminism, once institutionalized, has the potential to be as
authoritarian as any other institution (Derrida 1987). No
group is immune from preoccupations with origin and identity. On-going scrutiny and keeping on one's toes, is better

Hillary

than entrenching any politics. No position is permanently viable, it always occurs at the risk of self-authorization and perhaps at the expense of marginalizing alternatives and alternate possibilities. Since this can't be avoided, an appropriate politics is one which negotiates. Derrida tries to adopt the position of the 'both and' – in this case, both support for gender studies and a simultaneous critical reflection on gender studies. Much of his emphasis on the importance of negotiation is overlooked by feminist critics who claim that his position is reactionary because of its qualified support for feminism. A different response to Derrida takes into account his plea for a politics that tries to negotiate rather than singling out only one of the 'branches'.

Let's take a moment to look further at what Derrida can also offer a political movement. Deconstruction has been important in some strands of feminism, particularly deconstructive methodologies for dislodging inherited ideas. For example, critical as she has been of Derrida, French feminist theorist Luce Irigaray shares with him a methodological approach to the history of philosophy, in which the distinction between declaration and description is invaluable as a feminist resource. Confronted with a history of philosophy, psychoanalysis and anthropology in which women have been devalued, or excessively idealized, Irigaray has demonstrated the inconsistency of such representations of women, and argues that these representations are unstable and undermine themselves.

Some interest in deconstructive approaches is also manifest in the work of prominent American feminist and queer theorist, Judith Butler. Butler argues that gender norms for behaviour, codes, habits and styles are themselves citations, iterations and reproductions of copies for which there is no

JUDITH BUTLER
IRIGARY

original. Some are considered natural women and men, while others are deemed 'unnatural' (to give a literal example, drag artists imitate the codes for gender and sometimes suffer the injury of being deemed unnatural). But so-called 'natural' gender can be thought of as a generalized version of drag performance. It involves the mostly non-conscious reproduction, citation, reiteration of gender norms. Butler destabilizes the hierarchical opposition between the true original, the natural woman, and the artificial copy, the drag performance. So-called natural originals are generalized versions of the stigmatized, artificial copy. She concludes that there is no true original for gender norms.

Butler argues that a gender norm is never fully present because it must be constantly repeated. Its meaning is suspended across these repetitions, and it is never definitively accomplished. Gender norms therefore take on-going shape by being constantly cited anew. Moreover, copies are always recontextualized. Every context resignifies new meaning and every context is itself ready to be recontextualized. In one discussion, Derrida suggests that 'nothing exists outside context' (Derrida 1988, 152). Accordingly, we might say of gender norms that they are in this – and in the previous senses we have considered – 'contextual' and 'textual'.

Butler suggests that the necessary reiteration of gender norms also exposes them to mutation and transformation. A slightly different copy is replicated by further copies that are always slightly different. Thus gender norms and behaviour inevitably change in society, whether or not this is intended by gendered individuals. This may be our 'chance', or good fortune, in relation to gender norms.

Derrida suggested that the depreciation of femininity, and the binarization of sex into male and female, could be deconstructed through the 'generalization' of femininity into 'multiplicity of sexually marked voices' or a 'mobile of non-identified sexual marks' (Derrida and McDonald 1997, 40), dispersed through all subjects. At one time, this led to his own interest in trying to 'write like a woman' (Derrida 1973, 299). But his most significant contributions to feminism arise more from his deconstruction of depictions of maternity, women and femininity in the history of ideas and particularly of political thought.

*The Politics of Friendship* (1997C) reconstructs the filial and fraternal metaphors at work in historical concepts of democracy and political union. The concepts of politics and citizenship that we have inherited are infused with sexually specific imagery of the similarity and reciprocity between male citizens, a model that barely tolerates cultural and sexual difference. Derrida asks whether this inhibits the role played by women in the polis, or the facility with which the union between women and between women and men can be considered political. He argues that, historically, the politics of friendship involves a '*double exclusion* of the feminine, the exclusion of friendship between a man and a woman and the exclusion of friendship *between* women' (Derrida 1997C, 290). There have been few models or historical images of solidarity between women as the foundation for citizenship, or of solidarity between women and men. Accordingly, Irigaray has argued that when women were finally enfranchised in the twentieth century, they took up a symbolic position as the equivalent of men. Their political participation is based on the exclusion of an alternative which has never yet been seen historically, a political presence as women, rather than in terms of a neutrality she suggests is really masculine equivalence. However, both Irigaray and Derrida stress that a 'sheer' exclusion of the feminine is impossible, and that a conflicted and self-undermining preference for the implicitly male homogeneity of political participants is to be found in the writings of the history of political philosophy.

Other feminists – Irigaray's work is significant in this respect – have argued that new metaphors for women's relationship to political community would be required for women to operate effectively within it. Though Derrida does not propose new meanings for femininity and masculinity, he has proclaimed, 'let us dream of a friendship which goes beyond this proximity of the congeneric double . . . "beyond the principle of fraternity"' (Derrida 1997C, viii).

Feminism is not more prone to narcissism and authoritarianism than any other ideology or political movement, and Derrida can seem over-persuaded that feminism's risks in this respect are more significant than its accomplishments. Nonetheless, he makes a case that feminism should be willing to concurrently engage in a deconstruction of feminism *as* an on-going form of feminism.

## 6

# THE CONTEXT OF COMMUNICATION

The relation of 'mis' (mis-understanding, mis-interpreting, for example) to that which is not 'mis-' is not at all that of a general law to cases, but that of a *general possibility inscribed in* the structure of positivity, of normality, of the 'standard': All that I recall is that this *structural possibility* must be taken into account when describing so-called ideal normality, or so-called just comprehension or interpretation, and that this possibility can be neither *excluded nor opposed*. An entirely different logic is called for.

Extract from Derrida 1988, 157

Rousseau believed there was a connection between the size of a community, its capacity for harmony, and the forms of communication possible within it. If a community was small enough, it was possible for its participants to see and hear each other simultaneously, and so to arrive at agreement through the immediate communication between the participants made possible by that physical proximity. He suggested, in other words, a connection between an ideal form of communication and an ideal form of community. Both involve an ideal of transparency and proximity: I am in the presence of another person, and I feel we share common understandings. This is the basis of an ideal relationship between us, based on agreement.

By contrast Derrida disagrees with those who adopt ideals of community based on an ideal form of communication. As an alternative he proposes that we adopt the 'law of the "mis"', arguing that any successful communication always contains the alternative possibility of its own failure. No matter how much I might appear to be in harmony with others, our exchange is marked by its containing the possibility of miscommunication between us. A new kind of ethics of discussion opens up: one would always acknowledge, even in moments of high confidence, or optimism, the possibility of the 'mis'. The aim would not be to eradicate it, but to negotiate with it, just as, in previous chapters, we have seen Derrida argue that we should negotiate with rather than disavow, the impossibility of a natural body, a natural maternity, a natural entitlement to land, and a desirable political position free from the risk of reproduced authoritarianism.

For Derrida this possibility of failure is the condition of any communication. For the contemporary German philosopher Jürgen Habermas, any attempt at communication or use of language (even if hostile), and even any mode of action, presupposes a horizon of meanings shared with others. We could not function or speak otherwise. Habermas derives from this point the view that inherent to our communicative practices is the orientation towards 'universal and unconstrained consensus' (Habermas 1971, 314): the possibility of an ideal speech situation of collective comprehension. There is a kind of pre-understanding shared by humans – even in contexts of the worst misunderstanding – of the criteria for successful understanding.

For Habermas, the acknowledgement of the possibility of success lies within communicative failures through the implicit recognition of shared criteria constitutive of our communicative practices. By contrast, for Derrida the inevitability of a degree of failure is implicit in (and Derrida argues, makes possible) communication. This failure of communication embedded in communication calls for the recognition that we might not fully share criteria for success, or might make a mistake about what is shared. For Habermas, the ideal of mutual understanding is implied in day to day language and actions. For Derrida, this ideal is an impossible phantom. The 'mis' of misunderstanding or miscommunication is not aberrant. The risk of the 'mis' is integral to the possibility of language, action and communication.

Derrida's comments on the 'mis' followed from his deconstructive reading of the British philosopher John Austin in *Limited Inc* (1988). In his *How To Do Things With Words* (1962), Austin describes forms of statements that 'do' rather than say, when an individual for example declares, marries, promises, christens. Language is sometimes thought of as serving a representative function (as when it seems that the word 'marriage' points to an event in the world, a wedding). Austin points out, however, that language can also act in a different kind of way. With the words, 'I promise', a promise has taken place. Some kinds of language perform actions. There seems to be a kind of immediacy to them.

Derrida, deconstructing this claim, points to the conditions Austin attaches to such performative language. Obviously, Austin notes, a promise or a ceremony does not take place when said by an actor on a stage. Nor is a marriage performed when the celebrant is not legally entitled to perform it. Austin could not have foreseen the relevance of this point some thirty years later. In the United States, same-sex couples have been participating in marriage ceremonies whose legality (in battles between individuals and states, between state and federal law, and in battles at the heart of religious institutions) is uncertain. It has become a matter of states versus federal rights. Do individual US states have the right to prohibit gay marriage? Do individual US states have the right to consider invalid gay marriages performed in other states? Provisionally, yes. As of 1996, the so-called 'Defence of Marriage Act' (DOMA) passed by Congress allows this, and denies federal legality of gay marriages. But will this stand? Many believe DOMA to be unconstitutional. On the other hand, there are moves from conservative groups for a constitutional amendment restricting marriage to heterosexual couples. Despite the fact that in a few states gay couples have been engaging in ceremonies that are both symbolic, and legal or provisionally legal, the marriages could neither be declared definitively 'successful' (the act may eventually be open to challenge by federal law or constitutional amendment) nor unsuccessful (since a marriage ceremony does take place, in addition to a symbolic gesture, or a gesture of commitment).

Discussing performative speech acts, Austin finds himself obliged to clarify that 'the *circumstances* in which the words are uttered should be in some way, or ways, *appropriate* . . . [F]or naming the ship, it is essential that I should be the person appointed to name her; for (Christian) marrying, it is essential that I should not be already married . . . it is hardly a gift if I *say* "I give to you" but never hand it over' (Austin 1962, 8–9). Though this is not quite the overt conclusion drawn by Austin, the performative is, apparently, context-dependent. Instantaneity is mediated by the frame or context it enfolds. The fact that I am not speaking with heavy irony to concurrently 'undo' my promise as I say it, nor performing a line on a stage interrupts with its contextuality the instantaneity of the promise. For Derrida, context enfolds the statement, either authorizing or de-authorizing it. Such authorization is never definitive. One need only pass a law that all marriages performed by actors on stages in the last decade shall be legally binding, and the status of those acts changes. In fact, Derrida describes performativity – the idea that some statements instantly perform an action with which they are at one – as a 'luxury of authority', because it is premised on the requisite right, the conditions and the power to 'produce a performative' (Derrida 2000, 468). The notion of performativity distracts attention from the importance of context. Rather, Derrida suggests that we should focus on the contextual conditions making possible a 'successful' (or in Austin's words 'felicitous') performative statement, or speech act. Derrida's point is not that there are no speech acts. Instead, the speech act is only able to take place in relation to what does not, in fact, 'belong' to it: in this case, contextual authority, the recognized legitimacy of the agent, and social law. Furthermore, every context would be enfolded by another context, so that the context is never stable, or definitively fixing of the meaning, legitimacy or 'success' of the performative in question. One context is provided by the actor on the stage, another by the laws governing the legal status of that actor's statements, another the overall changes in the law that might pertain, another the different cultural and legal regimes that might be applicable, and so on.

In his discussion, Austin also makes a distinction between felicitous and infelicitous – failed – speech acts. Speech acts that do not seem to be accomplished as intended might be deemed infelicitous. Austin had suggested that some forms of language operate in different kinds of ways, not as the communication of a thought, nor the representation of a 'thing', but instead as 'doing'. Derrida does not disagree. But he asks what it means to describe a stage actor's promise as infelicitous. This is not because he wants to suggest, contra Austin, that the stage promise is legally binding, but because he is interested in the status of context in Austin's work. It seems to play an important role in this question Austin raises of felicity. Moreover, the notions of felicity and infelicity seem to imply some view of how things 'should' have turned out. But in whose view? For Austin's point is not to depict speech acts as expressing intentions such as aims and hopes. A speech act in his terms either is, or it isn't – it is not clear what supports the notion of its 'felicity'. For this reason, Derrida suggests that

> performative communication once more becomes the communication of an intentional meaning, even if this meaning has no referent in the form of a prior or exterior thing, or state of things. (Derrida 1982B, 322)

Once Derrida has suggested that context invaginates – a Derridean term for a sheath that enfolds the outside within – a speech act, he argues that the on-going possibility of its failure is present at the heart of every speech act, and – he expands this view – every other form of language:

> Austin's procedure is rather remarkable, and typical of the philosophical tradition that he prefers to have little to do with. It consists in recognizing that the possibility of the negative (here, the *infelicities*) is certainly a structural possibility, that failure is an essential risk in the operations under consideration; and then, with an almost *immediately*

*simultaneous* gesture made in the name of a kind of ideal regulation, an exclusion of this risk as an accidental, exterior one that teaches us nothing about the language phenomenon under consideration. (Derrida 1982B, 323)

For Derrida's critics, this was a copybook instance of Derrida paying insufficient attention to the author's intent: Austin wasn't especially interested in infelicity, and didn't consider the speech act to be the communication of intent. For these reasons he had suggested we should not be distracted by erroneous examples from his point of concern, such as the actor on the stage making a promise, or the person who goes through a marriage ceremony without being in a legal position to do so. Derrida, by contrast, was propelled into a fascination with what he defined as the general law of the 'mis'. The possibility of 'missing' – which relates to the perpetual possibility of an alternative context – inhabits 'successful' realization of speech acts, and more generally, the possibility of successful communication, even successful community, proximity or understanding.

In Derrida's view, should we look away from, or more closely at, the elements of a text that a writer considers marginal? Do we look more closely at, or politely turn our attention away from, Austin's actor on the stage or unauthorized marriage participation? In Derrida's opinion, we should look more closely. If we focus on such elements, Austin's text can be converted. His argument is transformed into something new and alien, something unexpected. Reading deconstructively, in other words, we can articulate the multiple possibilities associated with any speech act. Performative language, like any language, is dependent on its context. But the context itself is neither fixed, nor fully defined. Think of the ambiguity of gay marriage in the United States. We may think that the context will tell us if the speech act is felicitous or infelicitous. But there is no single context. There is the context of a couple's family and friends; the gay community and contemporary America. There is the perspective of this decade, and the retrospective perspective of this century to come. There is current state and federal law, which may not agree and so provide different contexts. According to the different ways in which we could think of the context, the gay marriage is many different actions (failed or successful) and can be read in many different ways.

Derrida also challenges the apparent instantaneity in contemporary western culture delivered through the media and new technology facilitating forms of communication and community. Western contemporary culture is depicted as global, faster, more instantaneous, even hyper-real. Community is considered drastically transformed by the age of the television, mobile phone and internet. Via such new media as blogs, Wikipedia, live and internet broadcasting, we access each other's ideas more readily. It seems that things happen at greater speed: transmission of data and communication, reporting. Derrida explores the way that the specific technologies of the time in which we live amount to an artifact (Derrida and Stiegler 2002, 3), a product of human art and craft. With this term he dislodges the effect of apparent immediacy, and the seductive impression that we see things 'live', or are immediately present to them through technology.

Instead, technology only generates the effects of instantaneity through technological means. Presence, actuality and instantaneity are 'effects' because they are mediated by such techniques. Televised events are selected for us by an editor. Derrida wants to dislodge the illusion of non-mediated instantaneity of images, facts and ideas. It is not that communication is 'just an illusion'. What is illusory is the artificial effect of unmediated pure immediacy. He also wants to dislodge another seductive but false belief relating to contemporary advanced technological culture, that such instantaneity and immediacy have only recently been made possible through contemporary technology.

A distant head appears in a screen in my living room, a far away voice on the telephone, data that would take me a great deal of time to gather in archives or libraries immediately appears at my fingertips thanks to the internet. Its apparent instantaneity is mediated by these contemporary technologies, yet there is a relationship here that has always been with us: the *fantasy* of immediacy and of the techne, or arts, that will accomplish it. Think of technologies that seem as rudimentary as the letter, the pencil, the edited discourse, the conventions followed by conversation around a table, the very fact of using clear syntax. They are arts that seem to close a geographical, temporal or interpersonal distance. We aspire to an immediate, small community of mutual comprehension, believe some impediment to communication stands in our way, and find promise in any mechanisms that might reduce that distance.

Derrida doesn't deny that between a pencil and the internet there are differences in the 'types' of technics. But we delude ourselves if we think there was a historical period in which simpler communities achieved a more natural immediacy. This is a long-standing fantasy, according to which (as Rousseau believed), greater understanding and consensus can be achieved in communities of small size and homogeneity stemming from the physical proximity of its members. As communities became large, impersonal and diverse, harmony of views, discussion amongst all participants, and the synchronicity of comprehension and physical presence became impractical. Notice how, in such a view, a progressively developing culture is considered a degradation. As modern life becomes more anonymous and complex, and the actual size of communities increasingly large, immediacy of all kinds becomes harder to attain.

The paradox of contemporary times is our belief that technology can restore for us lost immediacy: lost because we live in a complex and separated community. It seems to us that modern technology – air travel, the phone, the electronic chatroom – is able to bring us back together. But we never had the full community some like to think we lost. We were always at a kind of distance (geographical, emotional, political, generational, cognitive) from each other. And we never accomplish the instantaneity we think is promised by new technologies. The camera, the computer, the television, the instant survey result that seem to bring us together also seem to stand between us. Derrida deconstructs our idea that there is a perfect or ideal presence interrupted by some kind of impediment of distance or social division that could be expunged by arts, whether the pen or the internet.

Instead, he argues that the social bond itself supposes or requires interruption. Derrida acknowledges that this kind of refrain prompts many to think of his work as nihilist, or a menace to the political (Derrida 1998C, 224) as he doesn't believe in the ideal of community as 'a harmonious group, consensus, and fundamental agreement beneath the phenomena of discord or war' (Derrida 1995A, 355). By contrast, Derrida believes some degree of incomprehension and non-communication (the spacing, differentiation or *différance* at the heart of communication) to be inherent to communication. It is to be embraced, not deplored, since the latter erects an impossible ideal of full transparence to each other, and deems us 'fallen' in relation to that ideal.

If communication is understood to importantly contain non-communication, and community to include distancing and spacing, then rather than elevating impossible or implicit ideals, Derrida suggests a new ethics of negotiation would be produced. Incomprehension and dissemination are also to be respected, not overcome: they represent important, and not only negative differences within a community, and within the individuals constituting community.

This view of community has been extremely influential for a group of contemporary post-Derridean political philosophers including Jacques Rancière (1995), Jean-Luc Nancy (1986) and Iris Marion Young (1991). The ideal of community is not that we understand each other – or ourselves – perfectly. If harmony and social synchronicity are values, there is also value in the ways in which someone may greatly exceed my power of comprehension and anticipation or indeed, surprise themselves. Impossibilities of communication and community are both inevitable, and on occasion, usefully affirmed.

OBAMA.

# 7

## MOURNING AND HOSPITALITY

We know that there are numerous what we call 'displaced persons' who are applying for the right to asylum without being citizens, without being identified as citizens. It is not for speculative or ethical reasons that I am interested in unconditional hospitality, but in order to understand and to transform what is going on today in our world.

So unconditional hospitality implies that you don't ask the other, the newcomer, the guest to give anything back, or even to identify himself or herself. Even if the other deprives you of your mastery or your home, you have to accept this. It is terrible to accept this, but that is the condition of unconditional hospitality: that you give up the mastery of your space, your home, your nation. It is unbearable. If, however, there is pure hospitality, it should be pushed to this extreme.

I try to dissociate the concept of this pure hospitality from the concept of 'invitation'. If you are the guest and I invite you, if I am expecting you and am prepared to meet you, then this implies that there is no surprise, everything is in order. For pure hospitality or a pure gift to occur, however, there must be an absolute surprise. The other, like the Messiah, must arrive whenever he or she wants. She may even not arrive. I would oppose, therefore, the traditional and religious concept of 'visitation' to 'invitation': visitation implies the arrival of someone who is not expected, who can show up at any time. If I am unconditionally hospitable I should welcome the visitation, not the invited guest, but the visitor. I must be unprepared, or prepared to be unprepared, for the unexpected arrival of *any* other. Is this possible? I don't know. If, however, there is pure hospitality, or a pure gift, it should consist in this opening without horizon, without horizon of expectation, an opening to the newcomer whoever that may be. It may be terrible because the newcomer may be a good person, or may be the devil . . .

It is still a very profound lesson that Husserl taught us, and even Levinas. In the fifth *Cartesian Meditation*, Husserl insists that there is no pure intuition of the other *as such*, that is; I have no originary access to the alter-ego *as such*. I should go, as you know, through analogy or ap-presentation. So the fact that there is no pure phenomenon, or phenomenality, of the other or alter-ego as such is something which I think is irrefutable. Of course, it's a break within phenomenology, with the principle of phenomenology, and it is within the space opened up by this break that Levinas found his way. I think this is true, but it doesn't mean we have to subscribe to the whole context of Husserl's statement. However, if we take this simple axiom or principle, the principle which betrays the principle of phenomenology, and keep this apart from phenomenology, it is still valid for me. Now you can transport this statement into another context, which Levinas does, and which I shall do, too. But when I have to explain pedagogically to students what Levinas has in mind when he speaks of the 'infinity of the other', of the infinite alterity of the other, I refer to Husserl. The other is infinitely other because we never have any access to the other *as such*. That is why he/she is *the* other. This separation, this dissociation is not only a limit, but it is also the condition of the relation to the other, a non-relation as relation. When Levinas speaks of separation, the separation is the condition of the social bond.

Extract from Derrida 1998B, 70–1

In late works such as *Of Hospitality* (2000), Derrida makes a distinction between unconditional hospitality, which he considers impossible, and a hospitality which is always conditional. Hospitality has been a tradition in many cultures. In ancient Greek times, the stranger could often expect shelter in a household or city. The eighteenth-century German philosopher Immanuel Kant argued that individuals had a universal right to shelter in any country, but for a limited time period and not if they would jeopardize the security of the country in question. In contemporary times, nations admit a certain number of immigrants – conditionally. Admission may be subject to the lottery system, as in the United States, or to the display of particular needed skills, or to demonstration of wealth, or it may (as in the 1999 Australian reception of refugee Kosovars) be a temporary haven only, with immigrants not attributed the right to query the quality of the hospitality offered, or it may be subject to an immigrant's demonstrated risk of persecution in their home country. Derrida is one of many who question the excessively restricted nature of national hospitality to legal and illegal immigrants.

A distinctive aspect of Derrida's approach is his reflection on how absolute hospitality is impossible. When we try to imagine the extremes of a hospitality to which no conditions were set, we realize it could never be accomplished. This is not so much an ideal: it is an *impossible* ideal. The reader might think that this impossibility is so obvious as to be without interest, but Derrida argues that it has an important relation to conditional hospitality.

I may be the most practically hospitable person, yet I won't leave my door open to all who might come, to take or do anything, without condition or limit. We'd say the same of a nation – Derrida notes there is no nation-state in the world, to his knowledge, that allows thoroughly unconditional immigration. What is the relationship between this conditionality and the impossibility of a 'pure' hospitality? Derrida argues that acts of conditional hospitality take place only in the shadow of the impossibility of their ideal version. The admission by a country of a certain number of immigrants in a given year only occurs *as* the impossibility of an absolute hospitality, a limitless opening of national borders in which all property would be available to those who enter, and all doors would be open. Derrida doesn't think this impossibility is meaningless. The official who determines the admission quota can only do so by considering whether it should be larger, and judging that it should not. This is an engagement with the prospect of 'more' that resides within the limit established. This reflection is, at times, quite literal. Derrida quotes former French minister of immigration Michel Rocard who stated, with respect to immigration quotas, that France couldn't offer a home to everybody in the world who suffered (Derrida 1999A, 116). In the same moment that he shuts it down, Rocard opens up a conceptual possibility. For a brief moment, one sees a glimpse of an alternative absolute, an unconditional hospitality fended off by conditional hospitality.

Derrida is interested in unconditional hospitality in 'order to understand and to transform what is going on today in our world'. In his later work, he is interested in many unconditionals: such as an unconditional gift, an unconditional pardon and an unconditional mourning. As each of these is deemed 'impossible', impossibility takes on an increasingly strong resonance in his late work. I'll consider his reading of the gift, pardon, mourning and the messianic in this and the next chapter, and ask what political and ethical contribution a philosophy of impossibility can make.

Derrida's views on hospitality illuminate a transition in his philosophical project from earlier work such as *Dissemination, Of Grammatology* and *Limited Inc.* In his later work, there is some degree of shift with regards to ideals, and also some difference in his depiction of the other. In every Derridean reading we have considered so far (of Plato, Rousseau, Saussure, Austin, of depictions of maternity, gender, nature, community and family values in popular culture) an 'ideal' version is considered impossible. Derrida stressed that there could never be an ideal body, or maternity, or femininity; there could never be original nature or full understanding. In his early work impossible ideals are phantoms for which some of us are nostalgic or hopeful or from which we seek guidance. As such, they are deconstructed by Derrida. But in the material to which we now turn, Derrida stresses impossibility in a different way and makes a different use of the idea that ideals are impossible. This impossibility takes on a poetic function and amounts to an 'alterity' or 'otherness' with which we have an everyday relation as when Rocard's immigration quota is set through a mediation with a threshold of impossibility. In Derrida's work impossibility is not something that provokes idealization, nostalgia or abasement. Instead, it can open us up to possibilities of transformation. This may seem an odd example, since in the case of Rocard, it apparently did not. Yet his peculiar statement draws attention to itself. It draws attention to the fragility of its brutal authority. Some listeners might respond with quick agreement. But others might be provoked: why not? Why not more and better hospitality? What does set the limit?

Notice, in the above excerpt concerning hospitality, Derrida's comment that 'unconditional hospitality implies that you don't ask the other, the newcomer, the guest to give anything back, or even to identify himself or herself'. Such comments are a transformation of his discussion of otherness in classical philosophers such as Plato and Rousseau. From his earliest work, Derrida is concerned with the treatment of the other. In *Dissemination*, he describes the *pharmakon* as the 'combat zone between philosophy and its other' (Derrida 1981A, 138). Plato's *pharmakon* (like the Rousseauist supplement) is a self-contradicting term. The 'other' in this case is a term such as 'writing' that is devalued or 'made other' by classical philosophers so as to promote certain terms (such as thought or speech) as more original. We have seen Derrida's counter-argument that the exterior lies at the heart of the interior, that 'the meaning of the outside was always present within the inside' (Derrida 1997B, 35). Thus, otherness is also that which mediates identity. Derrida uses 'otherness' in this sense in *Dissemination*, referring to writing as 'the play of the other within being' (Derrida 1981A, 163). Similarly, we've seen him argue with Saussure that language signs are traced by *différance*, or otherness.

But in the above excerpt, Derrida is discussing otherness in reference to 'the other, the newcomer, the guest'. He interrogates our ethical relationship with other humans. How are we receptive to and in relationship with others: strangers, foreigners, immigrants, friends, loved ones? His discussion of mourning provides a tool for thinking about this question.

Derrida begins with the death of someone we know. Someone dies or abandons us – how shall we envisage the mourning that must be undergone? For a long time it may seem we cannot get over them. Mourning seems to be a kind of 'abnormal' period, in which the other lives within us:

> If death comes to the other, and comes to us through the other, then the friend no longer exists except *in* us, *between* us. In himself, by himself, of himself, he is no more, nothing more. He lives only in us. But *we* are never *ourselves*, and between us, identical to us, a 'self' is never in itself or identical to itself. This specular reflection never closes on itself; it does not appear *before* this *possibility* of mourning. (Derrida 1989, 28)

For mourning to fully succeed, we should be able to get over the loss of the other in question. But if we can get over him or her, something seems to have failed in the mourning. Think of how an easy recovery from a death feels like a betrayal of the person lost. From this perspective, a truly appropriate mourning would be a mourning we couldn't accomplish, that continues until our death. Derrida claims that if mourning succeeds, it fails, and it must fail in order to succeed. In this sense, mourning is impossible. Derrida's aim is not to berate those who have managed to recover from the loss of their loved ones. He has written many essays in which he mourns friends, family and colleagues. Never is his point merely 'academic'. Many who've lost loved (or hated) figures might well say that one dreads (and knows to be impossible) 'fully' getting over someone, just as one also dreams of it.

Derridean mourning also returns to his discussion of identity and difference. Derrida does not envisage humans as self-enclosed individuals different to each other. I am not fully autonomous of my friend in life, nor am I autonomous of them in the wake of their death. I can never thoroughly take my leave of the other, because I was never fully independent from the other. In a perfect mourning, we'd fully get over the other: but this belies the fact that we are always in relation with the (dead or alive) other.

In the opening excerpt Derrida alludes to an important distinction between messianicity and messianism, another way of reading his 'impossibility' and related notion of alterity. A messianism (waiting for the arrival of the Messiah) is considered by him a kind of dogmatism, subjecting the divine other to 'metaphysico-religious determination' (Derrida 1994, 89). When imagining the coming of the Messiah it attributes a new kind of origin and centrism to a divine other and assumes the latter suits our imaginative picture. In contrast, Derrida suggests invoking messianicity: as 'the unexpected surprise . . . If I could anticipate, if I had a horizon of anticipation, if I could see what is coming or who is coming, there would be no coming' (Derrida 2001B, 67–8). Derrida's view of messianicity is not limited to a religious context, but extends to his depiction of otherness more generally. His comments about the other apply to a friend, someone culturally different, a parent, a child;

where the issue arises of whether we are capable of recognizing them, of respecting their difference, and of how we may be surprised by them.

Adequately recognizing difference therefore may arise as an ethical imperative when relating to another culture, or to the many cultures in one country, or to the child, or friend. In all these instances, it is not uncommon to consider that another has been 'failed' if we assume that they are like us. Indigenous peoples and different cultures sometimes make claims for the recognition of cultural specificity; children make claims to be recognized as distinct and different to their parents; friends and lovers often resist the supposition arising between them that experiences and ideas are shared. Assuming the other to be the same to me, or, assuming they are reducible to my experience of them, is from this perspective an ethical failure.

If so, Derrida responds by pointing out that we are also unable to encounter the other *as* radically foreign. The other is always to some extent understood by my horizon of expectation. No matter how much we might take ourselves to be receptive to the other, our experience of another is always somehow restricted to our perceptions, our preconditions, our history. In *this* sense (but we must pay attention to the special meaning of impossibility in Derrida's work), the other may be described as 'impossible' for me.

The idea that alterity is – in the Derridean sense – impossible seems to run counter to the intentions of a 'philosophy of difference'. This is a point on which critics get stuck: this depiction of otherness seems to make the other a self-enclosed autonomous entity. It seems to propose fundamental substance (as if it had some kind of reality) in the otherness of the other, a problem with which negative theologians are preoccupied. Derrida seems to imply we are unable to be unconditionally hospitable to a radical other. Yet recall in his development of mourning that he seeks alternatives to the depiction of self-enclosed subjects as autonomous of each other. This is the source of critics' concerns. How does Derrida's treatment of the impossibility of the other avoid a return to the depiction of subjects and others as self-enclosed from each other?

His manner of treating impossibility offers a solution to the problem. According to Derrida, impossibility is an experience or an event. It is a relationship we have, which means that we could never be self-enclosed identities. Impossibility is not a possibility that I cannot access. Rather, I am differentiated by impossibility, and this is one of the many ways in which I am a being in relationship with otherness. When the country's borders, or the home's domain are open to guests or immigrants, conditional hospitality places us in *relation* to impossibility. We fail a greater generosity, and that impossible greater generosity inhabits our act of conditional hospitality. When, with the best intentions in the world, I nonetheless inevitably fail in my attempt to be open to the other's difference, that impossibility resides in my attempt, and places me in a different kind of relation with the other in question. It is not that impossibility performs no 'work': it mediates me, and contributes to the complexity of my identity.

How can this produce transformation? It is partly a matter of how we negotiate with impossibility. Consider again those government statements that reasonable limits and reasonable conditions must be set on immigration. Derrida is interested in the interconnection between overt institutional generosity and its implicit failure, 'when those hosts who are apparently, and present themselves as being, the most generous, constitute themselves as the most limited' (Derrida 1999A, 116). The French president Mitterrand once used the expression of a 'threshold of tolerance' (*seuil de tolérance*) in his discussion of immigration policy. This was considered the point beyond which French voters would revolt against the presence of immigrants in France. France was willing to admit a certain number of immigrants. Even if this was an act of national generosity it is incapable of accomplishing this generosity without invoking rhetorically a spectre of impossibility, that which is beyond its threshold. Politicians ask voters to accept this notion of the threshold, but the term 'threshold of tolerance' asks more questions than it answers. It opens up to the limits of that threshold, and the prospect (though deemed impossible) of exceeding it. The authoritarianism of this notion reflects its unstable nature. The closure of thought this allows is already inhabited by the limitation implied in the statement.

Declared closure can be converted by the deconstructive reader into an imagination of what may lie beyond that demarcated threshold. This is what Derrida's work on hospitality, mourning, and messianism contributes to thinking. The authoritarian assertion of the threshold provokes both positively and negatively the imagination on the part of those who contemplate the chance of a step beyond it. The deconstructive intervention points out that it was the French government's authoritarianism that described a prospect counter to its declarations whereby we imagine hospitality beyond the 'threshold'. Aren't we implicitly engaged in such a reflection, the moment that a threshold is articulated? This provides a good example of the form Derrida's reflections on transformation take. The capacity to read former Minister Rocard and former President Mitterrand's statements otherwise may be unsatisfying to the reader who looks for proposals for action aimed at social change. But it is not that Derrida's work is intended to supplant the latter. Derrida offers a means of reading. We return to an authoritarian statement, intended to close itself down to a more generous immigration policy. Derrida suggests a means of revising that statement so that it converts into a reflection, despite itself, about the possibility of a more generous immigration policy. This seems to me the kind of point on which Derrida's readers divide. It is rather like the actor on the stage considered in the previous chapter. When the author asks us to look away from the actor, do we take this advice literally, or follow Derrida's suggestion that it offers us the occasion to look closer and transform the meaning of that actor? When Minister Rocard announces that we cannot give shelter to everyone who suffers, do we consider his dogmatism as unmovable, or do we actively try to convert it into an implicit reflection on alternative possibilities: at the limit, giving shelter to everyone who suffers. Some – perhaps more literal minded readers – see no promise in the latter. Others are fascinated by the way that M. Rocard's statement deconstructs itself, drawing itself to alternative possibilities and performing far more imaginative work than the speaker would admit. Do we read 'for' such imaginative possibilities entrapped within politicians' worst statements? Or do we turn away from them? Do we convert them into strange, unexpected gestures, through Derrida's project of making the familiar appear alien to us? Do we find as much literalness in the statements with which we are bombarded, or do we find as much non-literality as possible? Derrida offers one more means of enriching one's political and social world, finding multiple and alternative layers of meaning in the flattest statement.

# 8

## GIVING AND FORGIVING

For there to be a gift, there must be no reciprocity, return, exchange, countergift, or debt. If the other *gives* me *back* or *owes* me or has to give me back what I give him or her, there will not have been a gift, whether this restitution is immediate or whether it is programmed by a complex calculation of a long term deferral or difference [*différance*]. This is all too obvious if the other, the donee, gives me back *immediately* the same thing . . .

For there to be a gift, it *is necessary* [*il faut*] that the donee not give back, amortize, reimburse, acquit himself, enter into a contract, and that he never have contracted a debt . . . The donee owes it *to himself* even not to give back, he *ought* not *owe* [*il a le devoir de ne pas devoir*] and the donor ought not count on restitution. Is it thus necessary, at the limit, that he not *recognize* the gift as gift? If he recognizes it *as* gift, if the gift *appears to him as such*, if the present is present to him *as present*, this simple recognition suffices to annul the gift. Why? Because it gives back, in the place, let us say of the thing itself, a symbolic equivalent.

Extract from Derrida 1992B, 12–13

Recognizing something as a gift raises the prospect of its potential reciprocation. If a gift depends on my expectation that the gift will be reciprocated, it is a kind of exchange, barter or trade. We have all experienced how a benefactor's desire for recognition is in inverse proportion to a gift. To the extent that I want someone to recognize me as the giver, I fail to live up to the impulse that I hope prompted the gift. To the extent that I expect reciprocation, the same is true. Extreme – though everyday – examples are easy to find. A man helps his children and tells them he expects to be helped in turn. The generosity of his help wanes. My friend gives me a beautiful gift, and I panic at its expense. Must I return in kind? We already enter this anxious relationship the moment I recognize I have been given a gift. But a gift has no meaning without being identified as such. At the extreme, a gift would have to not be a gift, to be a gift. Thus, Derrida – repeating a phrase which resonates throughout his work – suggests its conditions of possibility amount to its conditions of impossibility. He considers impossibility to be productive in the sense that it generates effects. He does not claim that gifts do not take place. Rather the event of a gift is generated through its own impossibility.

Derrida's later deconstructive reading of gifts varies from earlier work. His philosophy was founded on the widely used strategy of 'generalizing' the devalued term, in other words, finding a definition of the devalued term so broad that it can include the valued term opposed to it. This involves reading at the limit. One finds oneself with formulations where if writing is at a distance from the original idea, and is unreliable, isn't speech *at the limit* a form of writing? When writing about the gift Derrida no longer broadens the devalued term but he is again reading at the limit. If a gift is less a gift to the extent that recognition is required, *at the limit* wouldn't the pure gift be unrecognizable?

This sounds abstract. Yet Derrida's radical account of the impossibility of a 'pure' gift has some bearing on the day to day as we engage with the paradoxes Derrida describes. We know we undermine our gift if we resent its non-reciprocation, or expect the recipient to give something back – recognition, gratitude, equivalence.

Similarly, Derrida suggests that the pardon, or forgiveness, is impossible. True forgiveness would have to forgive the unforgivable. Derrida is amplifying our sense that something is amiss if forgiveness is too easily given. If the pardon is to count for something, we must be uncertain that we can be forgiven; the forgiveness must be hard won. If the forgiveness is too easily given there is no real forgiveness. We know that the easier we find it to forgive someone, the less forgiveness is worth. At the extreme, a forgiveness that costs and means nothing, hardly counts. The tougher, the more meaningful. Thus, perhaps only an impossible forgiveness – a forgiveness of that which can't be forgiven – would be a true forgiveness. Perhaps to the extent that it is forgivable at all, an act of pure forgiveness has not taken place. But since true forgiveness could only forgive the unforgivable, Derrida makes the leap to suggest true forgiveness is impossible (Derrida 2002A, 349).

When discussing 'the pardon', whether legal, political or personal, Derrida expands his definition of its impossibility. Are there any wholly innocent persons available to forgive crimes committed by and to humanity? Is there anyone thoroughly exempt who could judge, or forgive? Moreover, if one were to forgive someone on the condition that they repent and change, would one not be forgiving 'another' subject? True forgiveness of the 'subject in question' apparently would amount to my willingness to forgive an entirely unrepentant subject who would repeat their crime without hesitation and continue to do so. Such an impossible radical forgiveness would be the only 'true' forgiveness. Furthermore, in a true, radical or 'pure' forgiveness the person forgiving and the person forgiven would have to share a common understanding of the injury, crime or atrocity in question. But it is impossible that complete harmony of comprehension and experience could occur, just as it is impossible that any one subject could attain a definitive, self-identical and thoroughly resolved experience, understanding or memory of the event in question (whether they suffered or inflicted it). Derrida also mentions his discomfort at the sovereignty one assumes at the point at which one forgives. What do we assume about ourselves when we think we can forgive? No relation, descendant, state or collectivity can truly forgive on behalf of another. But can someone even forgive on behalf of 'themselves'? For one thing, the forgiving subject is not self-identical to the subject who suffered. A victim may not be in a position to forgive: they may have been deprived of speech, coherence or life. To forgive is, in a sense, to assert a sovereignty that rises above the incapacity to forgive. But 'pure forgiveness', Derrida suggests would be forgiveness without such self-appointed sovereignty. Pure forgiveness would involve forgiving what one was unable to forgive. Pure forgiveness is, for all these reasons, impossible.

Derrida's point is not to object to all impulses to give, forgive, welcome or mourn. Instead, he draws our attention to overly glib formulations of giving, forgiving and apology. In political contexts, national and governmental acts of apology have been all too numerous. They repeatedly fail to engage with the self-serving enhancement of sovereignty, or the appropriation of a victim's suffering, that can be at work in an apology that costs little. Derrida's interest in the relationship between conditional and (impossible) unconditional hospitality can also be seen in his reflections on government policies concerning immigration and political asylum. These are often depressingly conditional. When a government accepts those seeking political asylum, it is common to expect its recipients neither to question the nature of the hospitality, nor make any further demands. It is common for government representatives to make cynical public declarations that express the idealized values for which their country stands, and to vaunt national compassion and humanitarianism. The flagrant national self-identification, not to speak of the excessively conditional nature of the hospitality renders it no 'pure' hospitality. By stressing the impossibility of true hospitality, Derrida provokes our further reflection on constant failures constituted by conditional hospitalities.

One might wonder what kind of norm arises from Derrida's work. His lack of sympathy with particularly self-aggrandizing or uncircumspect gestures of forgiveness, hospitality and generosity (particularly those of institutions and nation states) is patent. A more predictable philosopher might have said that the best possible hospitality approximates maximally an ideal hospitality. This is not Derrida's position. Instead, Derrida would say that the best possible hospitality recognizes the impossibility of an ideal hospitality. Only from that position can it engage valiantly, eyes wide open, with a void. We must attempt the best possible hospitality we can accomplish in the *absence* of an ideal. This is a far more demanding politics. By contrast, the last thing the ministers of immigration of recent times in America, France, Britain and Australia have been willing to acknowledge is that we must do the very best we can in the avowed absence of inherent authority, or a legitimizing ideal. Instead, they elevate endless phantom ideals in phony self-justification: national harmony, respect for due process, or for thresholds of tolerance.

I know of no politician who has engaged overtly with deconstructive reflections of these kind. Yet Derrida's formulations could have resonance politically, in matters of policy, and in small ethical encounters at a daily level. We reside with otherness in the form of an impossibility that mediates or differentiates us. This can prompt complacency: that's to say, the self-satisfied personal or political certainty that one has been hospitable, given a gift, or satisfactorily forgiven. Such satisfaction is an inevitable failure. Instead, Derrida argues for a patient, attentive, negotiating relationship with the ways in which we inevitably fail the other. He isn't making a case for complacent acknowledgement of inevitable failure ('yes, yes, good friend, I know I fail you as I acknowledge you!'). One cannot justify a pitiful effort with the alibi that all hospitality is conditional anyhow. The ethics in question seem to be inherently uncomfortable (and yet Derrida does not have in mind liberal breast-beating). This is one reason that the term 'negotiation' works well: since one fails as one succeeds, one can only go on trying to listen for and respond to the failures that must accompany any possible successes. This is an ongoing practice.

Deconstructive concepts of responsibility and negotiation have proved influential in postcolonial politics and theory. For example, consider the work of contemporary writers such as Gayatri Chakravorty Spivak and Homi Bhabha. One problem addressed by Spivak and Bhabha is whether cultural difference is representable. In colonial contexts – in law, literature, correspondence and administrative policy – peoples of India and

Africa have been represented as the opposite of, or alternatively as 'like' the European. Either way, cultural difference is considered translatable, comprehensible, communicable to and with the European, as opposite or same. There is also failure in representations of a colonized other when he or she is deemed 'not like' the European. Such representations are too close to the racist conventions which imagine the racial other as inscrutable. This dilemma is apparent, for example, in debates over land rights in Australia. There is a problem if the relation of indigenous peoples to Australian land is assumed to be unlike western models of property ownership. It is equally problematic if the relation is assumed to be the same as a western model. The former may not adequately secure land rights reform despite the recently established legal view that indigenous peoples were illegally deprived of their land. The latter assumes that all peoples are alike and fails to do justice to cultural difference. One realizes that each strategy (stressing translatability, stressing untranslatability, using the very concept of translatability) fails. Confronted with such dilemmas, Spivak proposes that the most responsible position arises from a 'negotiating' position. Sometimes one must coordinate between, alternate, or simultaneously manipulate such strategies. But this representation is 'impossible' in a specific, deconstructive sense. Success fails, and failure succeeds.

At times it might be strategic to represent, as far as possible, the feelings, thoughts, intentions, needs, traditions, political demands, cultural specificity of a colonized or disenfranchised people. At times it might be critical to *also* stress the ways in which an individual or a people cannot be thoroughly represented or translated in traditionally European language or terms, nor, indeed, in any language. At different times, one or the other strategy might be provisionally 'best', but there is nothing definitive about what is deemed 'best'. Even if it has not been formulated through presumptuousness, dogmatism or idealization, a strategy is not exempt from disturbing sacrifice and loss. If one finds oneself representing what a person or people wants, says, desires, knows, intends, there is also an ethical claim to try to simultaneously articulate what cannot be said, or is lost, or fails. The result is a deliberately ambivalent politics committed to the ceaseless negotiation and making complex of its own position.

In his analyses of nineteenth-century colonial India, Homi Bhabha argues that cultural domination is intertwined with an ambivalence about the colonial presence and hybridity on the part of the colonized. He analyses the dissemination of the bible by British missionaries. Though this certainly is an instance of the hegemony of the British, the latter is also destabilized by British anxiety that they were unable to control, for all their efforts, the meaning of the bible amongst so-called natives. Attention to ambivalence and hybridity allows us to identify fractures in and resistance to the 'power and presence' of the English in colonial regimes such as nineteenth-century India. But ambivalence, hybridity and mimesis do not mitigate or minimize cultural domination. One needs, in stressing domination, to stress resistance, and in stressing resistance, to stress domination. These are the uncomfortable, on-going facts of deconstructive responsibility.

In 1994, Gayatri Chakravorty Spivak discussed the form taken by debate at the European Parliament in Strasbourg concerning the Bangladeshi Flood Action (FPA) Plan, through efforts of the Green party. The FPA was intended to provide flood control by technical intervention into the Bangladeshi river system, funded by the G7 through World Bank coordination. Spivak is known for her argument that the colonized subject cannot be heard. Willing, however, to negotiate that position, she comments 'because we have less power than the World Bank, and because some of us are of colour, when we confront the World Bank, we sometimes claim that the subaltern speaks' (Spivak 1994, 58). Her analysis is not that activists should have avoided this forum. Yet the imperative is to constantly stress the failure accompanying any success. Her analysis continued to evoke the silencing of the subaltern in this context. The meeting retained marginal status, and representations of the proceedings in an internal World Bank memo were dismissive. Bangladeshi speakers practised at such conventions were dismissed as seasoned professionals, 'the standard characters'. Meanwhile a middle-class Bangladeshi farmer unfamiliar with the conventions of such meetings was dismissed as a laughable and incomprehensible figure.

When the question arises of what a deconstructive politics amounts to, we might turn to Spivak's definition: 'deconstruction can make founded political programmes more useful by making their inbuilt problems more visible' (Spivak 1989, 206). In the above instance, one can stress the failures of speech that occur with successful 'open debate'. Similarly, one might support such NGO declarations of 'the right to self-determination', while making their inbuilt problems more visible. We can note that such a right 'will not touch the entire spectrum of Asian aboriginals' nor 'the cultural absolutism' of many of its groups (Spivak 2004, 543). So she concludes, 'The supplementary method that I will go on to outline does not suggest that human rights interventions should stop' (Spivak 2004, 550). It can only provoke an attentive politics, willing to press a bit further on the points of failure.

Consider a final example. Programmes to spread literacy in rural, poor areas in India have had some success. When images of girls in classrooms learning with smiles proliferate in testimony of the programme, the correct question to ask is 'what fails?'

Spivak, involved locally in some of the rural schools, analyses the differential nature of the literacy in question. At worst, she suggests, one identifies a kind of class apartheid. Repeatedly, the form of learning disseminated in the poorest schools is rote learning supported by inferior texts compared with the middle-class education focus on comprehension as a pedagogical tool.

The spectre of rote learning is also discussed by Derrida in relation to Plato. This present example clarifies the stakes of that earlier discussion. The issue is not whether spoken or written, rote or 'comprehension' methods are favoured in relation to the dissemination of knowledge. When Derrida deconstructs Plato he finds that rote learning is devalued to support a phantom idealization of spontaneous knowledge. What of Spivak's devaluation of rote learning? How should we read her hierarchy between understanding and rote learning which arises in a formerly colonial context of educational quasi-apartheid in conjunction with divisions between the privileged and underprivileged in India? Spivak's devaluation of rote learning is different to Plato's devaluation. In contemporary India, rote learning is sometimes considered good enough for the poor. Indeed, the marginalization of the poor sustains the hierarchy of privilege. The right to literacy is enfolded with an unspoken politics concerning appropriate forms of knowledge and education.

Yet, as Spivak writes, 'one cannot write off the righting of wrongs. The enablement must be used even as the violation is renegotiated' (Spivak 2004, 524). The education programmes also correct a previous violation of rights. Certainly the literary programmes should be honoured for their success. But this shouldn't diminish one's willingness to read for their failure. The correction of a rights violation might *also* amount to the perpetuation of another rights violation. Spivak associates deconstruction with the kind of responsibility we might locate in an attentive politics, rigorously seeking out an articulation of what is wrong with a success and a renegotiating of the violations. Practically, this would mean support for literacy programmes, in conjunction with the willingness to identify failure in success through a deconstruction of the oppositions, comprehension versus rote, and privileged versus underprivileged. This is different to a politics of supporting success while identifying failures in the system. Instead, it is a matter of recognizing that an advance may be simultaneously success and failure. This is a philosophical point whose conceptual outline can be framed by Derrida's formulation of the impossible gift and of a politics of forgiveness. Rather than thinking that the failure subtracts from the success, one might support the success at the same time as one recognizes the possible simultaneous failure. The alternative model supposes that there might be an ideal success, in which all weak points had been eradicated. Instead, a success might simultaneously encompass a failure. It may be impossible to achieve land rights without an ironing out of cultural difference. This may not mean there is a more ideal form of land rights in which that uniformity did not occur. It is rather a matter of being attuned to that homogenization, and trying to be responsive to it without taking this as an argument for less, or different, land rights. Spivak's argument may seem a little different, since one can certainly hope for a better form of education in the poorest schools. Yet there may be no form of education reform that does not find some way of reaffirming divisions between the privileged and the underprivileged. One can imagine that the stress on comprehension rather than learning by rote could lead to new divisions in its application in schools. Spivak's politics of negotiation expects that each success is at the same time some kind of failure, and argues for an on-going responsibility in this respect, rather than complacency with regards to the identification of success.

# 9

## JUSTICE AND THE LAW

The structure I am describing here is a structure in which law [*droit*] is essentially deconstructible, whether because it is founded, constructed on interpretable and transformable textual strata (and that is the history of law [*droit*], its possible and necessary transformation, sometimes its amelioration), or because its ultimate foundation is by definition unfounded. The fact that law is deconstructible is not bad news. We may even see in this a stroke of luck for politics, for all historical progress.

Extract from Derrida 1992A, 14

Many legal systems appear to protect their citizens from the chaotic alternative of unfettered violence through the rule of law. When a robber steals, a kidnapper imprisons, or a murderer takes a life they break the law, incurring the intervention of the police and courts. We assume that the difference between legality and illegality is the difference between a peaceable community sharing a basic social accord versus the spectre of unregulated brutality and force by its members. Yet the decisions of judges and the actions of law enforcement officials can result in individuals being deprived of their liberty, possessions and, in some countries, their life. The opposition between legality and illegality can not be aligned with the opposition between violence and non-violence, nor between law and violence. Instead, the law actually distinguishes between legitimate and illegitimate violence. We accept that the actions and decisions of police and judges may, on occasion, be violent – but legitimately violent. This prompts the following question: how can we be sure legitimate violence is different to illegitimate violence? When American judges uphold constitutional law, it is reasonable to interrogate the founding of the American constitution. When the police uphold the will of the nation, it is reasonable to interrogate the legitimacy of that nation. Presumably all forms of *legal* violence (law enforcement, imprisonment, the death penalty) are fundamentally justified by the legitimacy of the state in whose name they take place, which in turn confers legitimacy on its law enforcement officers.

The problem with seeking legitimacy in the state is that under scrutiny 'all States', Derrida suggests, 'have their foundation in an aggression of the *colonial type*' (Derrida 2001C, 57). The Australian example could provide the archetype, the 'legitimacy' of Britain's 1770 claim to Australian land ensured by its being made by James Cook by authority and in the name of King George III. In 1788 the British dispossessed indigenous peoples from land they appropriated. In the 1970s, Paul Coe from the Wiradjuri people and others challenged the legitimacy of this original dispossession at the Australian High Court, and in 1992 after a new challenge by Eddie Mabo and the Murray Islanders, the High Court found that Australia had not been 'terra nullius' ('land not under any sovereignty' or 'territory belonging to no one') at the time of the British claim.

The founding of all nations, Derrida claims, relies on some kind of similar gesture. In the twentieth century, one of the ruses of the apartheid regime was seen when H. F. Verwoerd relied on the creation of so-called 'self-administered', 'semi-autonomous' homelands for two-thirds of (black) South Africans, who were through that measure denied South African citizenship. As Australia was founded through the denial of rights to its indigenous people, South African apartheid denied suffrage to the majority of its people through a declaration that they are not 'its' people (and the principle of universal suffrage and free elections was endorsed through this exclusion). Derrida's question is always: in the name of what? As he notes of South Africa's apartheid regime, the 1948 Charter of the Institute for National Christian Education claims that it is God who wants 'nations and peoples to be separate'.

His essay 'Declarations of Independence' (Derrida 1986B) analyses the legitimacy of the American declaration of independence of 1776. Though founding legal documents are the bedrock of American law, they are neither legitimate nor illegitimate, signed as they are by signatories who in signing, retrospectively authorize themselves as agents who, by virtue of the declaration, 'will have been' authorized to sign it. The legitimacy of the declaration is therefore founded in paradox. Derrida has argued that legal regimes tend not to admit the instability of their own foundations. The American declaration of independence offers an excellent example. Paradoxically, alongside wording which stresses the founding nature of the document, the signatories also claim its prior legitimacy. The document does not confess the absence of any overarching legitimacy for its declaration of rights. Instead, it makes reference to an anterior, divine and natural authority. The signatories write that they 'assume among the powers of the earth, the separate and equal station to which the Laws of Nature and of Nature's God entitle them'. The declaration continues that it is their 'Creator' who has endowed them with 'certain unalienable Rights'. The 1789 French 'Declaration of the Rights of Man and of the Citizen' also claims rights it proclaims to be 'natural' and 'sacred'. The legal traditions of South Africa, Australia, the United States, and many other countries, both those with a literally colonial history, and those with a history of 'self-institution' of its own legal regimes prefer to appeal to a divine, natural or royal authority for legitimacy, as opposed to admitting that the state is founded arbitrarily.

Derrida's writings on legal authority have been influential on legal specialists, and the discipline of critical legal studies. Deconstruction of the law can pinpoint contradictory or self-undermining ideas within the legal tradition, important legal texts, or judgements. Clare Dalton, a US critic, argued in 1985 that contract law – governing legally enforceable promises – is founded on dualities: contract law is considered more private than public, more objective than subjective, and more concerned with form than substance. Dalton argues that these dualities mirror power structures in society 'which contribute to the inconsistency and substantial indeterminacy of contract doctrine'. She primarily criticizes the incoherent application of contract law to non-marital partner relationships in the 1980s. Where it was supposed that there had been some form of private agreement between the partners, a judge's decision was deflected away from recognizing that such arrangements were always infused with ideas and power relations belonging to the public domain. These might include stereotypes about the division of labour, goods and wealth between women and men. The social norm of such stereotypes meant that the implicit agreements could not quite count as a private arrangement between the individuals. Dalton made a persuasive case that the ideal of 'privacy' in the 'private' arrangement between two persons was always upheld – privacy was a lurking and idealized phantom invoked by a judge but never quite 'present': 'The court's creation of categories of contract of varying degrees of privateness is therefore only a strategy of displacing and containing, not resolving, the public threat to the private world of contract' (Dalton 1985, 1001). Such a reading allowed Dalton to make a controversial but influential critique of the unjust treatment of female de facto spouses in decisions that turned on the notion of the private implicit agreement. Another example is Duncan Kennedy's deconstruction of Sir William Blackstone's landmark commentaries on common law in England (2001/1755–8) and its distinction between rights and wrongs. Blackstone was concerned to achieve consistency with legal precedent, and restrict excessive variability in legal decisions. Kennedy analyses contradictory ideas where servitude is presented in Blackstone as freedom and finds a contradiction between a perception of the law as representing social bonds that are necessary to freedom, and the law as encroaching on individual freedom (Kennedy 1979). Janet Halley's *Don't*, to give another example, analyses homophobic treatment of homosexuality in US law and military policy based on the 1986 Bowers v. Hardwick decision, which decided that the constitutional right to privacy did not extend to sodomy between same-sex males. It is similarly interested in the contradictory ideas rife in the legal treatment of homosexuality in the United States.

The influence of Derrida's work on legal studies is strongly seen in the critical analysis of contradictory laws, legal judgements and legal regimes. That legal regimes are demonstrably grounded in vagueness has given renewed vigour to the critics of specific laws. Thus, Derrida has suggested that the deconstructibility of the law may be a 'stroke of luck' for politics (Derrida 1992A, 14). These analyses are often functional; rather than contenting themselves with demonstrating that certain laws or legal regimes are somehow founded in contradiction, the critic rather turns sustained attention through close textual analysis to exactly how homophobic law is maintained through its contradictions, or exactly how contract law prejudicial to women is sustained through its reference to the private 'implied' contract, or exactly how common law repeats its tensions between concepts of freedom and servitude.

Derrida departs from the perspective of Dalton, Kennedy and Halley, whose analysis of legal contradictions indicate the law's openness to criticism with regards to its treatment of women or homosexuality. None of these scholars makes the case that a perfect legal regime would be free of contradictory interpretation, but neither go so far as Derrida's 'affirmation' of undecidability. At the limit, Derrida's argument is that the law can be neither just nor unjust: it must be predictable, but it cannot be entirely predictable. He notes that the law won't affirm or negotiate openly with this 'trial' through undecidability. Instead, it becomes all the more authoritarian, as when it appeals to natural, divine or royal right, or to the oppositions between public and private, or it elevates the ideal of consistency and precedent.

Derrida introduces a distinction between law and justice. We want the law to be more than legal; we want it to be just. There have been occasions when legal disobedience seems appropriate in relation to laws and regimes that strike us as fundamentally unjust, as in American's antebellum and subsequent Jim Crow regimes, or the South African apartheid regime. There are times when judges are obliged to carry out or apply the terms of a law they publicly declare unjust, such as the 'three strikes' law of California and many other American states.

The law is inhabited by the prospect of a justice that it might, or might not accomplish. There is nothing especially controversial about Derrida's distinction between law and justice. Where the law is associated with 'legitimacy or legality, [that which is] stabilizable, and statutory, calculable, a system of regulated and coded prescriptions' (Derrida 1992A, 22), Derrida associates justice with that which is 'infinite, incalculable, rebellious to rule and foreign to symmetry, heterogeneous and heterotropic'. But we can track a transition in Derrida from his early to his late work based on his reference to undecidability.

In his early work, invented terms such as *différance* or 'found' terms such as '*pharmakon*' or 'supplement' were presented as exceeding such oppositions as speech/writing, presence/absence, and identity/difference. Derrida defined these terms which were neither presence nor absence, neither identity nor difference, as 'undecidable'.

Justice is also defined in terms of undecidability but, imagining it as a kind of excess or alterity that inhabits law, Derrida gives a new wealth of meaning to that notion of excess. Derrida suggests that legal decisions are neither just nor unjust. To be just, the law must conform with precedent, calculation, norms, yet not in a slavish fashion. Following an unjust law, even with impeccable legality, will not make it just.

Derrida admitted that the term 'justice' gave him a great deal of trouble, and he often commented that he was trying to think through the way in which he wanted to use the term. Certainly, he doesn't envisage justice as an identifiable doctrine or principle. Derridean justice fits into Derrida's discussions of impossibility, where Derrida attempts to use the idea of impossibility in a specific and productive way. For a pure justice to be possible, he argues that it would have to occur in a language in which all the subjects concerned are supposedly 'competent, that is, capable of understanding and interpreting . . . the violence of an injustice has begun when all the members of a community do not share the same idiom throughout . . . In all rigour this ideal situation is never possible' (Derrida 1992A, 17–18). The impossibility of a 'pure' justice does haunt or 'ghost' those legal decisions that are taken. So Derrida proposes that justice is an experience of the impossible. Many of our impulses – the impulse to criticize a current regime, our attempts to improve it, or the impulse of deconstruction – occur in the name of something we think of as justice. This is an intriguing phenomenon once we empty, as Derrida does, the term justice of any calculable content.

Derrida likens the structure of justice to that of the gift. Bringing together the terms, he writes of an 'idea of justice' that 'seems to be irreducible in its affirmative character, in its demand of gift without exchange, without circulation, without recognition or gratitude, without calculation and without rules, without reason and without rationality' (Derrida 1992A, 25). In his later work, Derrida points out that we are responsive to imperatives (Improve! Deconstruct! Give!). We assume that these occur under the umbrella of a formula of ethics of why one should give, or what justice amounts to. But the pure version of the imperative would occur without that content. Derrida arrives at this suggestion from his point, made elsewhere, that if we give because we know we should, or we feel obliged, or we recognize we are in a cycle of reciprocity, our gift does not count as a gift. At the limit, a gift would not be given as a gift, and would not be recognizable as such. It would be a kind of imperative 'Give!' without rationale or sense. It would be a kind of mad giving. Similarly, Derrida suggests that a pure impossible justice would have an element of madness to it. Yet he suggests that this impossible, pure justice somehow has resonance for us, that we try to improve or deconstruct in the name of justice which is sometimes – as he acknowledges at one point – a kind of blind faith. It is helpful to remember that Derrida's ideas concern an impossible pure gift, or pure justice. He doesn't call into question gifts that are given every day, or that we act in the name of a justice to which we can perfectly well account. The difficult point is his view that such acts *also* contain within them – importantly and significantly – a faith in justice which is contentless, 'impossible' and yet is at work.

Derrida's own work on the deconstructibility of law goes beyond a preoccupation with the law's contradictory thinking and vague foundations. He emphasizes instead the importance of recognizing the incalculability and 'undecidability' of law. Compare with Blackstone, for example, whose aim is to make the law as calculable and predictable as possible. Though this is what we most often expect from the law, Derrida nonetheless emphasizes the simultaneous importance of the undecidable factor in legal decision-making:

A decision that didn't go through the ordeal of the undecidable would not be a free decision, it would only be the programmable application or unfolding of a calculable process. It might be legal; it would not be just . . . the ordeal of the undecidable that I have just said must be

> gone through by any decision worthy of the name is never
> past or passed, it is not a surmounted or sublated (*aufge-*
> *hoben*) moment in the decision. The undecidable remains
> caught, lodged at least as a ghost – but an essential ghost
> in every decision, in every event of decision. (Derrida
> 1992A, 24)

In 'Force of Law', Derrida argues that a legal decision that
was entirely machine-like would be troubling. If it were only
'the programmable application or unfolding of a calculable
process', we might not associate a legal decision with justice,
even if it were fully in conformity with the law. Derrida suggests that we want a legal precedent or constitutional
interpretation to be freely reaffirmed in a judicial system. A
legal decision should go through a so-called 'trial of undecidability'. It must conserve the law – we find unacceptable a
decision that disregards it – yet if it slavishly follows precedent
or legal documents, it shows too much regard for the law. The
suggestion is that a law can't be entirely regulated, nor can it
be thoroughly unregulated. To be just, the law must, but can't
entirely, exceed mere conformity with precedent, calculation
and norms. Perhaps the most satisfying legal decision would
'destroy it or suspend it enough to have to reinvent it in each
case, rejustify it at least, reinvent it in the affirmation and the
new and free confirmation of its principle' (Derrida 1992A,
23). It could be argued that we need a middle point between
rigid legal regulation and anarchic absence of legal regulation.
Instead, Derrida argues that we want something impossible
from the law; that it be 'both regulated and without regulation' (Derrida 1992A, 23). This is the kind of contradictory
thinking that, in his deconstruction of law, is amplified by
Derrida into a kind of impossible necessity. What does it

mean for legal decision-making that must take place? These decisions are, Derrida concedes, urgent, so he stresses that a legal decision could be seen as a kind of event that 'happens'. It can partly be predicted, but it is uncertain exactly what will take place. To some extent, the urgency of the moment overtakes the rational assessment of the decision-maker and the decision is taken 'in' him or her, rather than 'by' him or her. This can sound abstract, and yet we have all had the experience of decisions about which we have long deliberated and which are taken with a degree of spontaneity. The decision one takes rarely occurs at random, and yet it is not uncommon that the split-second decision is capable of surprising even oneself.

# 10

# PERFECTIBILITY

'Democracy to come' does not mean a future democracy that will one day be 'present'. Democracy will never exist in the present; it is not presentable, and it is not a regulative idea in the Kantian sense. But *there is the impossible*, whose promise democracy inscribes – a promise that risks and must always risk being perverted into a threat. There is the impossible, and the impossible remains impossible because of the aporia of the demos: the demos is at *once* the incalculable singularity of anyone, before any 'subject', the possible undoing of the social bond by a secret to be respected, beyond all citizenship, beyond every 'state', indeed every 'people', indeed even beyond the current state of definition of a living being as a living 'human' being, *and* the universality of rational calculation, of the equality of citizens before the law, the social bond of being together, with or without contract, and so on. And this impossible that *there is* remains ineffaceable. It is as irreducible as our exposure to what comes or happens. It is the exposure (the desire, the openness, but also the fear) that opens, that opens itself, that opens us to time, to what comes upon us, to what arrives or happens, to the event. To history, if you will, a history to be thought completely otherwise than from a teleological horizon, indeed from any horizon at all. When I say 'the impossible that there is' I am pointing to this other regime of the 'possible-impossible' that I try to think by questioning in all sorts of ways (for example, around questions of the gift, forgiveness, hospitality, and so on), by trying to 'deconstruct', if you will, the heritage of such concepts as 'possibility', 'power', 'impossibility', and so on.

Extract from Derrida with Giovanna Borradori 2003, 120

Deconstruction has been widely influential in many disciplines, but generally, elements have been lifted out and converted to diverse purposes. It has been different things to different disciplines. In the context of maths and science studies, undecidability and endless differentiation have been among the most significant ideas (Plotnitsky 1994). Elizabeth Wilson points out the importance of deferring and differing to psychological and neurological theories of memory and the psyche (Wilson 1998). In the case of genetic research, Derrida stresses the instability around human essence. In architecture and fashion, deconstruction's influence seems to have been in dismantling or inverting basic elements of construction. Woody Allen's film title *Deconstructing Harry* (1997) means the term in the sense of 'breaking down' or 'understanding the dissonant elements of which Harry is composed' – giving up on a presentation of Harry as a unified individual.

The paradox at the centre of Derrida's work is that we must read and familiarize ourselves with the works of such figures as Plato, Rousseau, and Saussure to grapple with his ideas, yet as we take note of Derrida's readings those figures change in his hands. Simultaneously, his own philosophy draws on fragments of those who have come before. Those familiar with the history of philosophy recognize many figures; close readings and fragments of Heidegger, Kant, Levinas and Husserl amongst others continue to reverberate through the late work. Scholars are able to follow the way in which he picks up an idea (the status of the other in Husserl's fifth *Cartesian Meditation*, of the messianic in Benjamin, of justice in Levinas, of death in Heidegger), and slightly borrows from it, slightly changes it, in what he describes as a relationship of 'light displacement'. Derrida gleans and amplifies fragments of ideas. He has had a relationship of borrowing to the history of philosophy, and many other fields of inquiry have had an appropriative relationship to his work.

When he wrote his essay 'Force of Law', Derrida's project (transformed by some of his readers into critical legal studies) was starting to seem thoroughly practical. He does not disavow these applications, but he goes out of his way to introduce elements that unsettle our understanding of deconstruction. Just when legal scholars became interested in the late 1980s in the project of deconstructing law, Derrida introduced an element that has caused a great deal of difficulty to the idea that he had become more 'applicable' to social and political contexts: the decision and its relationship to undecidability.

Derrida distinguishes the kind of banal day to day decisions from an event that might qualify as a pure decision: the latter would be radically unpredictable, and incalculable. If it could be predicted, or calculated, Derrida states that the event would fall short of what he imagines as 'the pure decision'. We can determine and predict the conditions of my decision to buy milk, the calculation through which I arrive at that decision, and the likelihood with which I will carry it out.

The process leading to many (certainly not all) legal decisions is similar. In addition to such easily determinable decisions, Derrida suggests that in legal and all other contexts it is useful to think of a pure 'impossible' decision. It would be radically incalculable, radically unpredictable. Of course, urgent decisions are often taken by us, and Derrida also stresses that even 'incalculable justice *requires* us to calculate' (Derrida 1992A, 28). But in addition to the banal decisions taken daily, and the urgent decisions taken legally, and politically, there is also a kind of decision-making that occurs 'in us' rather than it being performed 'by us', and about which we could never know with certainty that a pure decision had not taken place: 'Who will ever be able to assure us that a decision as such has taken place? That it has not . . . followed a cause, a calculation, a rule?' (Derrida 1992A, 25)

One more time, Derrida makes deconstructive philosophy quite a foreign matter to deal with. Think of Derrida's comment in an interview with Richard Kearney about the project of deconstruction: 'My central question is: from what site or non-site (*non-lieu*) can philosophy as such appear to itself as other than itself, so that it can interrogate and reflect upon itself in an original manner?' (Derrida 1984, 108). We've seen his capacity to make such things as maternity, Plato, a legal decision, hospitality, immigration and the gift appear differently. Just as the point where deconstruction itself started to appear familiar, Derrida intervened to make his own work appear other to itself anew.

Derrida's comments on the impossibility of a pure decision interconnects with his discussion of the event. Just as Derrida distinguishes between everyday decisions, and an incalculable decision, he distinguishes between events that take place, and a pure event which would be entirely unexpected. He is interested in events that would do away with the understanding of the cause and effects of things. He comments that there would be a pure event only if there were no horizon of expectation for it (Derrida 2002A, 94). Derrida refers to events that have the capacity to surprise us a little – whether or not it rains this evening, for example (Derrida 2002A, 96) – or a lot, as in the fall of the Berlin wall. But he comments, 'the event cannot be reduced to the fact that something arrives' (Derrida 2002A, 96). He distinguishes events as something happening in the day to day sense from a pure event: not one we could have easily predicted, like the rain, nor one we might have predicted with difficulty, like German reunification, but one that is *purely* unpredictable. One example he gives is the exact moment of the wall's fall, as opposed to the general, anticipatory possibility that this could happen at some time.

Unexpectedly, what Derrida stresses is that although we may not be sure when or if an event has occurred, it is imaginable that purely unforeseeable events sometimes occur (Derrida and Roudinesco 2004, 52). This is depicted as an experience we could have of the impossible, but only barely:

> What arises unforeseeably, what both calls upon and overwhelms my responsibility . . . the event, the coming of the one who or which comes but does not yet have a recognizable figure . . . That is what an event worthy of the name can and ought to be, an *arrivance* that would surprise me absolutely . . . what arrives and comes down upon me, that to which I am exposed, beyond all mastery . . . in such a way that I don't see it coming . . . having to content myself with feeling or hearing it. But barely. (Derrida and Roudinesco 2004, 52)

Derrida envisages our radical passivity in relation to this pure event. If we return to his discussions of the pure gift, a pure hospitality, or a pure pardon, all unconditionals, we see in this late period evidence of his proposal that the impossible *may* happen. If so, it would be 'but barely'. Since it is difficult to follow this last phase in Derrida's work, let's consider another instance of his strange evocation of the 'but barely'. This time, Derrida is speaking of the possibility of what we know he has considered impossible, an unconditional hospitality:

I cannot regularly organize unconditional hospitality, and that's why, as a rule, I have a bad conscience, I cannot have a good conscience because I know that I lock my door, and that a number of people who [sic] would like to share my house, my apartment, my nation, my money, my land, and so on and so forth. I cannot regulate, control, or determine these moments, but it may happen, just as an act of forgiveness, some forgiveness may happen, pure forgiveness may happen. I cannot make a determinate, a determining judgement, and say: 'this is pure forgiveness', or 'this is pure hospitality', as an act of knowledge, there is no adequate act of determining judgement . . . but it may happen without even my knowing it, my being conscious of it, or my having rules for its establishment. Unconditional hospitality can't be an establishment, but it may happen as a miracle . . . in an instant, not lasting more than an instant, it may happen. This the . . . possible happening of something impossible which makes us think what hospitality, or forgiveness, or gift might be. (Derrida 2001B, 101–2)

Our problem is to understand the status of the *pure* hospitality, gift, forgiveness, or event, that, we are told, 'might' happen. Insofar as it is calculable, predictable or determinable, it would not count as a pure event. Previously Derrida pointed out that a pure hospitality is impossible. We saw his additional point that impossibility, in the Derridean sense, does not mean, 'pointless to think about'. The impossibility inhabits us with a troubling foreignness, that unsettles and operates as a kind of internal critique of the inadequate hospitalities (gifts, pardons) we do accomplish.

Now, in the late period, Derrida pushes things further. In addition to the ghosting of gifts, hospitalities, and pardons with foreignness, Derrida adds that impossibility (a pure event, a pure pardon, a pure hospitality) might happen, fleetingly, and without our full knowledge. If so, we would be passive in relation to it, and might not know it had happened, or, only barely. Derrida's idea is not to deny or minimize the importance of the gifts, pardons, events, hospitalities that we recognize and experience, but to stress that these do not cover the whole field. There must always be those pure events of which we are unaware or of which we are only barely conscious, and these may *also* be tremendously important to human life. Derrida offers some examples, and we can add others.

In a curious essay about his friendship with the philosopher Sarah Kofman, Derrida (2001A) introduces an allegory suggesting that despite the ways in which he and Kofman were almost impossible for each other (those close to both know it to have been a difficult relationship), they *may* have implicitly forgiven each other, but in a way that neither could identify or pinpoint. If there had been a mutual forgiveness, it is one of which neither could ever be sure. Certainly we are aware of most pardons. But some important forms of forgiveness between individuals might also be those that are difficult to put into words, that the parties in question might not directly recognize and might never be positive about. Difficult relations that become smoother over time, or, relations that remain as a difficulty but in which the parties somehow learn to negotiate the awkwardness can be like this. The point is not to substitute for the more common way we think about forgiveness, but to remember that the entire level of forgiveness does not reduce to specific instances of knowledge, certainty and recognition: it can be more inexpressible.

Perhaps the best thing is to 'respect difference', it is sometimes said. The difference of another's experience may be such that we cannot know what another feels, and must respect that their experience is radically unknowable by me. Without undermining this ethics of respect, we can also add to it. Respect for the other's difference should not be equated with the mistaken view that all difference reduces to issues of knowledge. The other's experiences can have an impact in ways about which one is not fully aware or articulate. This is, for example, often said of the children of survivors of extreme trauma, such as the children of holocaust victims. The child may rightly say she can imagine nothing of her parent's experiences. Yet her dreams, nightmares and fantasies, aspirations, expectations, demeanour and bodily comportment are likely to have been affected by them. The point is that knowledge and conscious or reflective experience are not the only level at which we impact on each other. This is not to question the politics of respecting the difference of the other, but to expand it. The difference of the other may have modified me long ago, in subtle ways one can hardly name. It is at the level of this kind of unspoken passage of experience between subjects that Derrida imagines the possibility of a pure gift, a mourning, a decision, a hospitality, or a form of forgiveness the participants might not be aware of, but which – just barely – could take place nonetheless.

At the time of his death in 2004, Derrida was also producing new work that involved the refiguring of progress. His often-mentioned triumvirate, Plato, Rousseau and Saussure share a preoccupation with purity: a pure linguistic system, not contaminated by writing, or a pure nature, not contaminated by culture, and purely ideal forms, autonomous of the human. In one of the most startling developments of his work, Derrida returned to the language of purity and perfectibility in his late work.

Some thirty years and thirty books after *Of Grammatology*, Derrida writes of an impossible purity, as when he writes of an impossible pure hospitality, or an impossible pure gift. Why isn't this a Derridean 'nostalgia' for impossible purity? This question gives us an opportunity to compare again and for a last time the early and late Derridas. In Rousseau's work, the purity of nature is depicted as the opposite of a fall; these two positions occupy a relation of polarity. What safeguards Derrida's work from returning to a pathos of the fall into culture, a fall in which the conditional versions of hospitality figured as degradations from the pure, unconditional hospitality? Derrida's safeguard is that he *affirms* the latter as impossible.

The consequences of his affirmation of ideals as impossible is that progress will also take on a new status. In much of his late work he makes reference to the notion of legal improvement and perfectibility, the supposition that progress can be unceasingly accomplished: a process for which Derrida has gone so far as to declare his love (Derrida 2001B, 100). The perfection or ideal, and the point of this process need not be based on its lover securing a finite point in which progress finally culminates, nor presupposing a finite, hypothetical horizon. According to its conventional principle, perfectibility involves constant and slowly accumulating progress. Yet if we make constant progress, the point to which we progress not only recedes but also transforms. We are infused with belief in progress, engaged in transformation without guarantee, anticipating a future from a present constantly refigured, so that every future must be the anticipation of another future. Derrida writes that 'For democracy remains to come . . . not only will it remain indefinitely perfectible, hence always insufficient and future, but, belonging to the time of the promise, it will always remain, in each of its future times, to come' (Derrida 1997C, 306).

Derrida emphasizes that the nature of perfectibility has to be *constantly* revised (Borradori 2003, 13–14). Perfectability is always in a state of 'infinite progress' (Derrida 2002E, 26). Since progress never stops, we are again in a domain in which Derrida describes transformation and alterity but no ideal, fixed, regulative, originating or culminating moment. While we continue to love the perfectibility that represents progress, that love must be radically refigured. We don't know into what, since the process is infinite. The references in Derrida's late work to perfectibility and progress therefore have a very specific status. These terms are not conceived as if they were an event in history. Derrida acknowledges that we imagine and perceive social improvement as progress. In addition to the kinds of changes that we importantly recognize as progress, we must also imagine a kind of 'pure progress'. It is impossible, because (to give just one reason) it would otherwise suppose a definitive moment in history – that moment could never come. However, if a pure progress can be theorized as impossible, one modification of Derrida's late work is his new stress that it could, barely, happen. If it did, we could not identify it as such, and would be passive in relation to it.

Derrida's own engagements, activities and the tone of his writing make clear that he is not calling for quietism. Rather, this radical passivity can be thought of as a kind of supplement rather than a substitution to daily activity. Rather than being passive in lieu of being active, we should appreciate that there will always be forms of event, change, surprise and progress that are beyond our scope of knowledge. If this were not so, all forms of significant progress would be reduced to those kinds we would be capable of identifying or instigating. As before, Derrida is proposing a kind of respect for the other, for what 'ghosts' or troubles our own zone of expectation and identification, rather than relinquishing our responsibility. It's a matter of saying: 'I must do my best', but I am also the site for events and decisions in relation to which I am passive. In this respect one can only be optimistic that the result will be the best, and not the worst. In some of his writings, Derrida stresses it might be terrible or monstrous.

Derrida's work on democracy embodies this notion of the 'barely there' possibility. His last work *Rogues* argues that the idea of democracy is always deferred and differs from itself. We'd expect the early Derrida to deconstruct such appeals to democracy, and discussing statements by contemporary politicians and public figures in America, *Rogues* does do so. But in line with the shift in his thinking Derrida here reminds us that democracy is ghosted by an impossibility: by a 'democracy to come'. In his early work, his intervention might have been accomplished by demonstrating that democracy is never definitively achieved, and by questioning the idealization of

America in its self-promoting devaluation of the 'rogue state'. But in the late work, Derrida both makes this point and makes a new kind of intervention. Though he had always argued that deconstruction is affirmative, it becomes more clearly legible as such. Democracy-to-come is not a pure ideal, it is an impossibility, but is also 'barely possible'.

Impossibility thus has an important, phantom-like relationship with us. We live, in significant ways, with the impossibility of a pure democracy. Might a different political life arise if we acknowledged this rather than disavowing it: if we fully assume the impossibility of the ideal version? And then, Derrida adds one more point. We are not masters of what happens, nor what comes. And impossible as democracy is, we lack the authority to say it could not come. We might not recognize it if it did. It is likely that it would not be what we expected. We would not have been responsible for its advent. We might not even know it had come. But just as we are not masters of the universe enough to arrange its final advent, neither are we masters enough to definitively establish that it could never come. After his early analyses of the ways a true surprise is impossible, Derrida went on to say a true surprise could – just possibly – happen. This was, in some ways, a surprise in his own work and a promise of work to come. Perhaps he saw it as a means of embedding in deconstructive politics what he hoped would be an anti-authoritarian impulse.

# CHRONOLOGY

**1930** Jackie Derrida born 15 July, El-Biar, Algeria.

**1942** Excluded from Lycée de Ben Aknoun. Anti-semitism and Pétain policy under German occupation of France zealously enforced in Algeria: Jewish students restricted to seven per cent at Ben Aknoun.

**1942–3** Enrolled at Lycée Emile-Maupas for segregated Jewish students and teachers.

**1948** Passes *baccalauréat* at Lycée Gauthier; undertakes *hypokhâgne* classes in Algiers leading to relocation to complete *hypokhâgne* and pursue higher studies in Philosophy in Paris.

**1952–3** Studies at Ecole Normale Supérieure.

**1957** Passes the *agrégation*, after consistently troubled student career (absences from school in 1942–3, failed *baccalauréat* in 1947, failed entrance examination for E.N.S. in 1949 and 1951, failed *agrégation* in 1955, related to nervous disturbances, depression, etc.)

**1957** Residency in America, auditor at Harvard, marries psychoanalyst Marguerite Aucouturier.

**1957–9** Military service, served through post as school teacher in Algeria during Algerian war.

**1962** Publication of his French translation of Edmund Husserl's *Origin of Geometry*. The 100-page translator's introduction is awarded the Jean Cavailles Prize in modern epistemology.

**1963** Birth of son, Pierre.

**1964** Takes up teaching post in History of Philosophy at the Ecole Normale Supérieure, retained till 1984, concurrent career of extensive visiting professor posts in the United States (Johns Hopkins, Yale, University of California at Irvine, Cornell University, City University of New York).

**1967** Birth of son, Jean. Publication of three crucial works, *Speech and Phenomena*, *Of Grammatology* and *Writing and Difference*.

**1970** Death of his father, Aimé Derrida (he and Derrida's family had relocated to Nice following Algerian independence).

**1972** Publication of second trio of crucial works: *Positions*, *Dissemination* and *Margins of Philosophy*.

**1974** Publication of *Glas*.

**1980** Defends his *Thèse d'Etat* at University of Paris 1 (Sorbonne) through presentation of a selection of his published works. Conference on his work organized in France (*Les fins de l'homme*). Publication of *The Postcard*.

**1981** Detained (on false charge of drug possession and smuggling) during teaching visit to dissident scholars in Prague; released within days through efforts of French president François Mitterrand.

**1982** French minister of Research and Technology gives Derrida a brief which will lead to the founding of a non-conventional institution (*Collège internationale de philosophie*) for philosophy and interdisciplinary seminars offered by French and international scholars outside the confines of the academic system (with free access to all, and no degrees bestowed).

**1983** Elected to new position at *Ecole des hautes etudes en sciences sociales*, Paris.

**1984** Son Daniel born to Sylviane Agacinski.

**1986** Collaboration with architects Bernard Tschumi and Peter Eisenman (associated with deconstruction in architectural theory) towards the design of a large-scale park in Paris, the Parc de la Villette. See other cross-disciplinary collaborations: appearance in the film *Ghost Dance* in 1982, video work *Plays* in 1987.

**1987** Publication of *The Truth in Painting*. Highly mediatized debates in which (at their most scurrilous) deconstruction was associated with fascist ideology because of articles published in a Belgian collaborationist newspaper from 1940–42 by Paul de Man (grouped with Derrida and other deconstructive literary scholars at Yale) and also following the publication of Victor Farias's *Heidegger and Nazism*.

**1991** Death of Derrida's mother Georgette Derrida.

**1992** Controversy over honorary doctorate from Cambridge University. Some members of the university (and a small group of international philosophers) protest. Derrida wins a university vote on the matter 336–204.

**1994** Publication of *Politics of Friendship*.

**1999** Release of Safaa Fathy's movie *Derrida's Elsewhere*.

**2001** Theodor W. Adorno Prize of the city of Frankfurt am Main.
**2002** Release of Kirby Dick and Amy Ziering Kofman's movie *Derrida*.
**2004** Publication of *Voyous*.
**2004** Dies of pancreatic cancer at the age of 74 on 8 October.

# SUGGESTED RESOURCES

*Website*

*www.hydra.umn.edu/derrida/*
This contains many primary texts by Derrida online and useful interviews.

*Movies*

Dick, Kirby and Amy Ziering Kofman (2002). *Derrida*.
Fathy, Safaa (1999). *Derrida's Elsewhere*.

*Collections of interviews and roundtable discussions*

Derrida presents his work clearly in interview and roundtable format.
Derrida, Jacques (1995). *Points . . . Interviews 1974–1994*. Ed. Elisabeth Weber. Trans. Peggy Kamuf et al. Stanford CA, Stanford University Press.
Derrida, Jacques (1997). *Deconstruction in a Nutshell*. Ed. John D. Caputo. New York, Fordham University Press.
Derrida, Jacques (2002). *Negotiations: Interventions and Interviews, 1971–2001*. Ed. and trans. Elizabeth Rottenberg. Stanford, CA, Stanford University Press.
Derrida, Jacques and Roudinesco, Elisabeth (2004). *For What Tomorrow . . . A Dialogue*. Trans. Jeff Fort. Stanford, CA, Stanford California Press.

*Biographies*

No conventional biographies have been published to date, but one can read Geoffrey Bennington and Derrida's joint publication, *Jacques*

*Derrida* (1993: Chicago, University of Chicago Press), which contains some autobiographical material from Derrida in a piece called 'Circumfession', Bennington's presentation of Derrida's work, an extensive chronology discussed with Derrida, family photographs, etc.

## Obituaries

Derrida's obituaries are an illuminating archive of the controversy surrounding his work, and are collected together at *www.hydra.umn.edu/ derrida/obits.html*. They include pieces by such prominent philosophers as Axel Honneth, Jürgen Habermas, Judith Butler, Etienne Balibar and Mark Taylor. One of the most informative, which provides an excellent overview of Derrida's work was published by Richard Kearney and Thomas Baldwin in the *Guardian*; see *www.iapl.info/NEWS/DER-RIDA/ GUARDIAN.htm*.

The website 'Remembering Derrida' includes links to the caustic obituary of Derrida's work published in the *New York Times* that provoked over 4000 signatories of protest; see *www.humanities.uci.edu/ remembering_ jd/*.

## Recommended anthology

Derrida, Jacques (1991). *A Derrida Reader*. Ed. Peggy Kamuf. New York, Columbia University Press.

## Introductions to Derrida

Gasche, Rodolphe (1986). *The Tain of the Mirror: Derrida and the Philosophy of Reflection*. Harvard, Harvard University Press.

Harvey, Irene (1986). *Derrida and the Economy of Differance*. Bloomington, IN, Indiana University Press.

Howells, Christina (1999). *Derrida: Deconstruction from Phenomenology to Ethics*. Cambridge, Polity.

Royle, Nicholas (2003). *Jacques Derrida*. London, Routledge.

The first three of the above explain Derrida from the perspective of the history of philosophy; Royle situates Derrida in the field of literary studies.

*On the ethical and political implications of Derrida's work*

Beardsworth, Richard (1996). *Derrida and the Political*. London, Routledge.

Bennington, Geoffrey (2001). *Interrupting Derrida*. London, Routledge.

Borradori, Giovanna (ed.) (2003). *Philosophy in a Time of Terror: Dialogues with Jürgen Habermas and Jacques Derrida*. Chicago and London, University of Chicago Press.

Critchley, Simon (1992). *The Ethics of Deconstruction: Derrida and Levinas*. Oxford, Blackwell.

Derrida, Jacques (1994). *Specters of Marx: The State of the Debt, the Work of Mourning, and the New International*. Trans. Peggy Kamuf. New York and London, Routledge.

Derrida, Jacques (2005). *Rogues: Two Essays on Reason*. Trans. Michael Naas and Pascale-Anne Brault. Stanford, Stanford University Press.

Sprinker, Michael (ed.) (1999). *Ghostly Demarcations: A Symposium on Jacques Derrida's Specters of Marx*. London, Verso.

*Derrida's late work (themes such as mourning, the gift, hospitality, messianicity)*

Caputo, John D. (1997). *The Prayers and Tears of Jacques Derrida*. Bloomington and Indianapolis, Indiana University Press.

Derrida, Jacques and Anne Dufourmantelle, (2000). *Of Hospitality*. Trans. Rachel Bowlby. Stanford, Stanford University Press.

Derrida, Jacques (2001). *On Cosmopolitanism and Forgiveness*. Trans. Mark Dooley and Michael Hughes. London, Routledge.

Krell, David Farrell (2000). *The Purest of Bastards: Works of Mourning, Art, and Affirmation in the Thought of Jacques Derrida*. University Park, PA, Pennsylvania State University Press.

Naas, Michael (2003). *Taking on the Tradition: Jacques Derrida and the Legacies of Deconstruction*. Stanford CA, Stanford University Press.

Rapaport, Herman (2003). *Later Derrida: Reading the Recent Work*. London, Routledge.

*On deconstruction in literature and literary theory*

Culler, Jonathan (1982). *On Deconstruction: Theory and Criticism After Structuralism*. Cornell, Cornell University Press.

Derrida, Jacques (1992). *Acts of Literature*. Ed. Derrick Attridge. New

York and London, Routledge. (An anthology of Derrida's writings on literature, with an excellent interview between Derrida and Attridge, '"This Strange Institution Called Literature": An Interview with Jacques Derrida'.)

See also the works of Barbara Johnson and Paul de Man, two of the most prominent deconstructive literary critics.

## On deconstruction and legal studies

Cornell, Drucilla, Rosenfeld, Michel and Carlson, David Gray (eds.) (1992). *Deconstruction and the Possibility of Justice*. New York and London, Routledge.

## On deconstruction and architecture

Wigley, Mark (1993). *The Architecture of Deconstruction: Derrida's Haunt*. Cambridge, MA, MIT Press.

See also the bibliography compiled by Eddie Yeghiayan relating to the theme 'Postmodernism and Beyond: Architecture as the Critical Art of Contemporary Culture' at *http://sun3.lib.uci.edu/~scctr/hri/postmodern/*

## Deconstruction and postcolonial studies

Bhabha, Homi K. (1994). *The Location of Culture*. New York and London, Routledge.

Spivak, Gayatri Chakravorty (1988). *In Other Worlds: Essays in Cultural Politics*. New York and London, Routledge.

## Deconstruction and gender and sexuality studies

Butler, Judith (1991). 'Imitation and Gender Insubordination', in *Inside/Out: Lesbian Theories, Gay Theories*. Ed. D. Fuss. New York and London, Routledge: 13–31.

Feder, Ellen K., Rawlinson, Mary C. and Zakin, Emily (eds.) (1997). *Derrida and Feminism: Recasting the Question of Woman*. New York, Routledge.

Holland, Nancy (ed.) (1997). *Feminist Interpretations of Jacques Derrida*. University Park, PA, Pennsylvania State University Press.
Irigaray, Luce (1985). *Speculum of the Other Woman*. Trans. Gillian C. Gill. Ithaca, NY, Cornell University Press.
Sedgwick, Eve Kosofsky (1990). *Epistemology of the Closet*. California, University of California Press.

## Deconstruction and religion

Derrida, Jacques (1986). *The Gift of Death*. Trans. David Wills. Chicago, University of Chicago Press.
Vattimo, Gianni and Derrida, Jacques (eds.) (1998). *Religion*. Trans. David Webb et al. Stanford, CA, Stanford University Press.

## Deconstruction and mourning

Derrida, Jacques (1989). *Memoires for Paul de Man*. Trans. Cecile Lindsay et al. New York, Columbia University Press.
Derrida, Jacques (2001). *The Work of Mourning*. Ed. Michael Naas. Trans. Pascale-Anne Brault. Chicago, University of Chicago Press.

## Deconstruction and autobiography

Derrida, Jacques (1985). *The Ear of the Other: Otobiography, Transference, Translation*. Ed. Christie McDonald. Trans. Peggy Kamuf and Avital Ronell. Lincoln, University of Nebraska.
Derrida, Jacques (1993). 'Circumfession', in *Jacques Derrida*. Geoffrey Bennington and Jacques Derrida. Trans. Geoffrey Bennington. Chicago, University of Chicago Press.
Smith, Robert (1995). *Derrida and Autobiography*. Cambridge, Cambridge University Press.

## On deconstruction, science studies and mathematics

Johnson, Christopher (1993). *System and Writing in the Philosophy of Jacques Derrida*. Cambridge, Cambridge University Press.
Johnson, Christopher (1998). 'Derrida and Science'. *Revue Internationale de Philosophie* 52 (205): 477–93.
Norris, Christopher (1997). *Against Relativism: Philosophy of Science, Deconstruction and Critical Theory*. Cambridge, MA, Blackwell.

Plotnitsky, Arkady (1994). *Complementarity: Anti-Epistemology After Bohr and Derrida*. Durham, NC, Duke University Press.

Wilson, Elizabeth (1998). *Neural Geographies: Feminism and the Microstructure of Cognition*. New York, Routledge.

# REFERENCES

Austin, John (1962). *How to Do Things With Words*. Oxford, Clarendon.

Blackstone, William (2001) (first pub. 1755–8). *Commentaries on the Laws of England*. Ed. W. Morrison. London, Cavendish.

Borradori, Giovanna (ed.) (2003). *Philosophy in a Time of Terror: Dialogues with Jürgen Habermas and Jacques Derrida*. Chicago and London, University of Chicago Press.

Butler, Judith (1999). *Gender Trouble: Feminism and the Subversion of Identity*. New York, Routledge.

Dalton, Clare (1985). 'An Essay on the Deconstruction of Contract Doctrines'. *Yale Law Journal* 94 (5): 997–1114.

Derrida, Jacques (1973). 'La question du style', *Nietzsche aujourd hui*. Paris, 1018.

Derrida, Jacques (1981A). *Dissemination*. Trans. Barbara Johnson. Chicago, University of Chicago Press.

Derrida, Jacques (1981B). 'Economimesis' (trans. Richard Klein). *Diacritics* 11 (2): 3–25.

Derrida, Jacques (1981C). *Positions*. Trans. Alan Bass. Chicago, University of Chicago Press.

Derrida, Jacques (1982A). 'Différance', *Margins of Philosophy*. Trans. Alan Bass. Brighton, Sussex, Harvester Press: 1–27.

Derrida, Jacques (1982B). 'Signature Event Context', in *Margins of Philosophy*. Trans. Alan Bass. Brighton, Sussex, Harvester Press: 309–30.

Derrida, Jacques (with Kearney, Richard) (1984). 'Deconstruction and the Other', in *Dialogues with Contemporary Continental Thinkers: The Phenomenological Heritage: Paul Ricoeur, Emmanuel Levinas, Herbert Marcuse, Stanislas Breton, Jacques Derrida*. R. Kearney. Manchester, Dover: 107–26.

Derrida, Jacques (1986A). 'But, beyond . . . (Open Letter to Anne McClintock and Rob Nixon' (trans. Peggy Kamuf). *Critical Inquiry* 13 (Autumn): 155–70.

Derrida, Jacques. (1986B). 'Declarations of Independence' (trans. Tom Keenan and Tom Pepper). *New Political Science* 15 (Summer): 1–15.

Derrida, Jacques (1987). 'Women in the Beehive: A Seminar with Jacques Derrida' (trans. James Adner), in *Men in Feminism*, eds. Alice Jardine and Paul Smith. New York, Routledge.

Derrida, Jacques (1988). 'Afterword: Toward an Ethic of Discussion' (trans. Samuel Weber), in *Limited Inc*. Evanston, IL, Northwestern University Press: 111–54.

Derrida, Jacques (1989). *Memoires for Paul de Man*. Trans. Cecile Lindsay et al. New York, Columbia University Press.

Derrida, Jacques (1992A). 'Force of Law: The "Mystical Foundation of Authority"' (trans. Mary Quaintance), in *Deconstruction and the Possibility of Justice*. D. Cornell, M. Rosenfeld and D. G. Carlson. New York and London, Routledge: 3–67.

Derrida, Jacques (1992B). *Given Time: 1. Counterfeit Money*. Trans. Peggy Kamuf. Chicago and London, University of Chicago Press.

Derrida, Jacques (1992C). *The Other Heading: Reflection on Today's Europe*. Trans. Michael Naas and Pascale-Anne Brault. Bloomington and Indianapolis, Indiana University Press.

Derrida, Jacques (1993). 'Circumfession' (trans. Geoffrey Bennington), in *Jacques Derrida*. G. Bennington and J. Derrida. Chicago, University of Chicago Press.

Derrida, Jacques (1994). *Specters of Marx: The State of the Debt, the Work of Mourning, and the New International*. Trans. Peggy Kamuf. New York, Routledge.

Derrida, Jacques (1995A). '"A 'Madness' Must Watch Over Thinking"', in *Points . . . Interviews 1974–1994*. Ed. Elisabeth Weber. Trans. Peggy Kamuf. Stanford CA, Stanford University Press: 339–64.

Derrida, Jacques (1995B). 'The Rhetoric of Drugs' (trans. Michael Israel), *Points . . . Interviews 1974–1994*. Ed. Elisabeth Weber. Stanford CA, Stanford University Press: 228–54.

Derrida, Jacques (1997A). *Deconstruction in a Nutshell*. Ed. John D. Caputo. New York, Fordham University Press.

Derrida, Jacques (1997B). *Of Grammatology*. Corrected edition. Trans. Gayatri Chakravorty Spivak. Baltimore and London, Johns Hopkins Press.

Derrida, Jacques (1997C). *The Politics of Friendship*. Trans. George Collins. London, Verso.

Derrida, Jacques (1998A). *Monolinguism of the Other or the Prosthesis of Origin*. Trans. Patrick Mensah. Stanford, CA, Stanford University Press.

Derrida, Jacques (1998B). 'Hospitality, Justice and Responsibility: A Dialogue with Jacques Derrida', in *Questioning Ethics: Contemporary Debates in Philosophy*. R. Kearney and M. Dooley. London and New York, Routledge: 65–83.

Derrida, J. (1998C). 'Fidélité à plus d'un'. *Cahiers Intersignes* 13: 221–65.

Derrida, Jacques (1999A). 'Responsabilité et hospitalité'. *Manifeste pour l'hospitalité*. Ed. M. Seffahi. Paris, Paroles d'Aube.

Derrida, Jacques (1999B). *Sur Parole: instantanés philosophiques*. Paris, Editions de l'aube.

Derrida, Jacques (2000). 'Performative Powerlessness – A Response to Simon Critchley' (trans. James Ingram), *Constellations* 7 (4): 466– 8.

Derrida, Jacques (2001A) '. . . (Sarah Kofman 1934–94)'. *The Work of Mourning*. Ed. M. Naas. Trans. Pascale-Anne Brault. Chicago, University of Chicago Press: 165–88.

Derrida, Jacques (2001B). *Deconstruction Engaged: The Sydney Seminars*. Eds. Paul Patton and Terry Smith. Sydney, Power Publications.

Derrida, Jacques (2001C). *On Cosmopolitanism and Forgiveness*. Trans. Mark Dooley and Michael Hughes. London, Routledge.

Derrida, Jacques (2002A). 'As If It Were Possible, "Within Such Limits" . . .', in *Negotiations: Interventions and Interviews, 1971–2001*. Ed. and trans. E. Rottenberg. Stanford, CA, Stanford University Press.

Derrida, Jacques (2002B). '"Dead Man Running": Salut, Salut', in *Negotiations: Interventions and Interviews, 1971–2001*. Ed. and trans. E. Rottenberg. Stanford, CA, Stanford University Press: 257–92.

Derrida, Jacques (2002C). 'The Deconstruction of Actuality', in *Negotiations: Interventions and Interviews, 1971–2001*. Ed. and trans. E. Rottenberg. Stanford, CA, Stanford University Press: 85–116.

Derrida, Jacques (2002D). 'Nietzsche and the Machine', in *Negotiations: Interventions and Interviews, 1971–2001*. Ed. and trans. E. Rottenberg. Stanford, CA, Stanford University Press: 215–56.

Derrida, Jacques (2002E). *Ethics, Institutions and the Right to Philosophy*. Trans. Peter Pericles Trifonas. Lanham, ML, Rowman and Littlefield.

Derrida, Jacques (2005). *Rogues: Two Essays on Reason*. Trans. Michael Naas and Pascale-Anne Brault. Stanford CA, Stanford University Press.

Derrida, Jacques and Dufourmantelle, Anne (2000). *Of Hospitality*. Trans. Rachel Bowlby. Stanford, CA, Stanford University Press.

Derrida, Jacques and McDonald, Christie V. (1997). 'Choreographies: Interview' (trans. Christie V. McDonald), in *Feminist Interpretations of Jacques Derrida*. N. Holland. University Park, PA, Pennsylvania State University Press: 23–42.

Derrida, Jacques and Roudinesco, Elisabeth (2004). *For What Tomorrow . . . A Dialogue*. Trans. Jeff Fort. Stanford, CA, Stanford California Press.

Derrida, Jacques and Stiegler, Bernard (2002). *Echographies of Television*. Trans. Jennifer Bajorek. London, Polity.

Habermas, Jürgen (1971). *Knowledge and Human Interests*. Trans. Jeremy Shapiro. Boston, Beacon Press.

Halley, Janet E. (1999). *Don't: A Reader's Guide to the Military's Anti-Gay Policy*. Durham: Duke University Press.

Jardine, Alice (1985). *Gynesis: Configuration of Woman and Modernity*. Ithaca, Cornell University Press.

Johnson, Christopher (1993). *System and Writing in the Philosophy of Jacques Derrida*. Cambridge, Cambridge University Press.

Kennedy, Duncan (1979). 'The Structure of Blackstone's Commentaries'. *Buffalo Law Review* 28: 205–382.

McLemee, Scott (2004). 'Derrida, A Pioneer of Literary Theory, Dies'. *The Chronicle of Higher Education* 51 (9): available at *http://chronicle.com/free/v51/i09/09a00101.htm*

Nancy, Jean-Luc (1991). *The Inoperative Community*. Trans. Peter Connor et al. Minnesota, University of Minnesota Press.

Plotnitsky, Arkady (1994). *Complementarity: Anti-Epistemology After Bohr and Derrida*. Durham, NC, Duke University Press.

Rancière, Jacques (1998). *Disagreement: Politics and Philosophy*. Trans. Julie Rose. Minnesota, University of Minnesota Press.

Saunders, George (2004). 'My Amendment'. *The New Yorker*. 8 March: 38–41.

Saussure, Ferdinand de (1974). *A Course in General Linguistics*. Trans. Wade Baskin. London, Fontana/Collins.

Searle, John (1983). 'The Word Turned Upside Down'. *New York Review of Books*. 27 October: 79.

Spivak, Gayatri Chakravorty (1989). 'Feminism and Deconstruction, Again: Negotiating With Unacknowledged Masculinism'. *Between Feminism and Psychoanalysis*. Ed. T. Brennan. London, Routledge.

Spivak, Gayatri Chakravorty (1994). 'Responsibility'. *Boundary 2* 21(3): 19–64.

Spivak, Gayatri Chakravorty (2004). 'Righting Wrongs'. *The South Atlantic Quarterly* 103 (2/3): 523–81.

Welleck, René (2005). 'Destroying Literary Studies', in *Theory's Empire: An Anthology of Dissent*. Ed. D. Patai and N. Corral. New York, Columbia University Press. First published in *The New Criterion* 2 Dec. 1983: 1–8.

Wilson, Elizabeth (1998). *Neural Geographies: Feminism and the Microstructure of Cognition*. New York, Routledge.

Young, Iris Marion (1991). *Justice and the Politics of Difference*. Princeton, Princeton University Press.

# INDEX

# CREDITS

*Dissemination* by J. Derrida, trans. Barbara Johnson, 1981; reproduced by permission of Athlone/The International Continuum Publishing Group. *Positions* by J. Derrida, trans. Alan Bass, 1981; reproduced by permission of Athlone/The International Continuum Publishing Group. *Monolinguism of the Other* by J. Derrida, trans. Patrick Mensah; copyright © 1998 by the Trustees of the Leland Stanford Jr University; English translation © 1996 Editions Galilee; used with the permission of Stanford University Press. *Of Grammatology* by J. Derrida, trans. Gayatri Chakravorty Spivak, 1998; reprinted by permission of the John Hopkins University Press. 'Signature, Event, Context' in *Margins of Philosophy* by J. Derrida, trans. Alan Bass, 1982; reprinted by permission of Pearson Education. *Limited Inc* by J. Derrida, trans. Samuel Weber and Jeffrey Mehlman, 1988; reprinted by permission of Northwestern University Press. *The Other Heading: Reflections on Today's Europe* by J. Derrida, trans. Pascale-Anne Brault and Michael B. Naas, 1992; reprinted by permission of Indiana University Press. *Memoirs for Paul De Man*, by J. Derrida, trans. Cecile Lindsay, ed. Jonathan Culler and Eduardo Cadava; copyright © 1989 Columbia University Press; reprinted with permission of the publisher. 'Hospitality, Justice and Responsibility' in *Questioning Ethics* by J. Derrida, ed. Richard Kearney and Mark Dooley, Routledge, 1998; reproduced by permission of Taylor and Francis Books Ltd. *Given Time* by J. Derrida, trans. Peggy Kamuf, Chicago University Press, Chicago, 1992; reprinted by permission of the publisher. 'Force of Law: "The Mystical Foundation of Authority"' by J. Derrida, trans. Mary Quaintance, in *Deconstruction and the Possibility of Justice*, ed. Druscilla Cornell, Michel Rosenfeld and David Gray Carlson, Routledge, 1992. *Philosophy in a Time of Terror*, ed. Giovanna Borradori, Chicago University Press, Chicago, 2003; reprinted by permission of the publisher. *Deconstruction Engaged: The Sydney Seminars* by J. Derrida, ed. Paul Patton and Terry Smith, Power Publications, 2001.